First World War
and Army of Occupation
War Diary
France, Belgium and Germany

35 DIVISION
Divisional Troops
Divisional Ammunition Column
28 January 1916 - 31 March 1918

WO95/2475/3

The Naval & Military Press Ltd
www.nmarchive.com
Published in association with The National Archives

Published by

The Naval & Military Press Ltd

Unit 10 Ridgewood Industrial Park,

Uckfield, East Sussex,

TN22 5QE England

Tel: +44 (0) 1825 749494

www.naval-military-press.com

www.nmarchive.com

This diary has been reprinted in facsimile from the original. Any imperfections are inevitably reproduced and the quality may fall short of modern type and cartographic standards.

© **Crown Copyright**
Images reproduced by permission of The National Archives, London, England, 2015.

Contents

Document type	Place/Title	Date From	Date To
Heading	WO95/2475/3 35 Div Jan'16-Mar'19 Div. Ammunition Column		
Heading	35th Division Divl Artillery. 35th Divl Ammn Column Jan 1916-Mar 1919		
War Diary	Bulford Camp	28/01/1916	01/02/1916
War Diary	Havre	02/02/1916	05/02/1916
War Diary	Arques	06/02/1916	09/02/1916
War Diary	Mametz	09/02/1916	18/02/1916
War Diary	Mametz-Haverskerque	19/02/1916	20/02/1916
War Diary	Haverskerque	20/02/1916	29/02/1916
Heading	35th D.A.C. Supplement to Vol. I.		
Miscellaneous	List of officers starting on Active Service with 35 D.A.C. 1st February 1916 from Bulford.	01/02/1916	01/02/1916
Heading	35th D.A.G. Vol I		
War Diary	Haverskerque	01/03/1916	08/03/1916
War Diary	Lt. Floris	09/03/1916	21/03/1916
War Diary	Haverskerque	21/03/1916	30/03/1916
War Diary	Doulieu	31/03/1916	16/04/1916
War Diary	Doulieu-Paradis	17/04/1916	19/04/1916
War Diary	Paradis	19/04/1916	14/05/1916
War Diary	Zelobes	15/05/1916	31/05/1916
Miscellaneous	Sub Division of Sections I II & III. A Echelon 35th D.A.C		
Miscellaneous	Sub Division of Section IV. B Echelon 35th D.A.C.		
War Diary	Zelobes	01/06/1916	19/06/1916
War Diary	Ecleme	20/06/1916	30/06/1916
Heading	War Diary 35th Division Ammunition Column R.F.A. 1st to 31st July 1916		
Heading	War Diary of 35 D.A.C. from 1st July 1916-31st July 1916		
War Diary	La Thieuloye	01/07/1916	04/07/1916
War Diary	Authieule-Bretel	05/07/1916	09/07/1916
War Diary	Authie	09/07/1916	12/07/1916
War Diary	Millencourt	13/07/1916	13/07/1916
War Diary	Bois De Tailles K.18 Cent. Sheet 62 D.	14/07/1916	20/07/1916
War Diary	F.26 a.2.1	20/07/1916	24/07/1916
War Diary	F.26.a.2.1 Map Ref. 62 D.	25/07/1916	31/07/1916
Heading	35th Divisional Artillery. 35th Divisional Ammunition Column. R.F.A. August 1916		
Heading	War Diary of 35. D.A.C. From Aug. 1.1916 to Aug 31. 1916 (Volume 7).		
War Diary	Map References 62D Filiforme Tree F26.A.2.1	01/08/1916	02/08/1916
War Diary	S. of Dernencourt E.27.a.5.2 Map Ref 62 D.	02/08/1916	31/08/1916
Heading	War Diary of 35 D.A.C from Sept 1. 1916 Sept 30.1916. (Volume 8)		
War Diary	S. of Dernancourt Map Ref. 62D E.27.a.5.2	01/09/1916	03/09/1916
War Diary	Daours	03/09/1916	03/09/1916
War Diary	Daours-Rainneville	04/09/1916	05/09/1916
War Diary	Rainneville-Boisbergues	05/09/1916	05/09/1916
War Diary	Boisbergues-Remaisnil	06/09/1916	07/09/1916

War Diary	Remaisnil-Lucheux	07/09/1916	07/09/1916
War Diary	Lucheux-Montenescourt	08/09/1916	08/09/1916
War Diary	Montenescourt	09/09/1916	15/09/1916
War Diary	Wanquetin	15/09/1916	30/09/1916
Heading	War Diary of 35 D.A.C from Oct 1.1916-Oct 31.1916. (Volume 9).		
War Diary	Wanquetin	01/10/1916	31/10/1916
Heading	War Diary of 35 D.A.C. from Nov. 1st 1916-Nov 31st 1916 (Volume 10).	01/11/1916	01/11/1916
War Diary	Wanquetin K 32 Sheet 51C N.E.	01/11/1916	30/11/1916
Heading	War Diary of 35 D.A.C. from Dec 1st 1916-Dec 31st 1916 (Volume 11).		
War Diary	Wanquetin K.32. Sheet 51 C N.E.	01/12/1916	26/12/1916
War Diary	Rebreuviette M.6 Central Sheet 51C.	27/12/1916	31/12/1916
Heading	War Diary of 35 D.A.C. From January 1st-January 31st 1917. (Volume 12).		
War Diary	Rebreuviette M.6 Central Sheet 51C.	01/01/1917	08/01/1917
War Diary	Bouret M.3.b.9.8. 51c	09/01/1917	14/01/1917
War Diary	Wanquetin K.32.c 51C N.E.	15/01/1917	31/01/1917
Heading	War Diary of 35 D.A.C. from Feb 1st-Feb 28th 1917 (Volume 13).		
War Diary	Wanquetin K.32.c. 51C N.E.	01/02/1917	04/02/1917
War Diary	Rebreuviette M.6 Central Sheet 51c	05/02/1917	07/02/1917
War Diary	Outrebois	08/02/1917	09/02/1917
War Diary	Bourdon	10/02/1917	18/02/1917
War Diary	Argoeuves	18/02/1917	18/02/1917
War Diary	Aubigny	19/02/1917	19/02/1917
War Diary	Hangard	20/02/1917	20/02/1917
War Diary	Ignaucourt V.27.B.7.5 Rosieres Combined Sheet	21/02/1917	28/02/1917
Heading	War Diary of 35 D.A.C from March 1-March 31st 1917. (Volume 14).		
War Diary	Ignaucourt V.27.b.7.5 Rosieres Combined Sheet	01/03/1917	17/03/1917
War Diary	Caix E.3	18/03/1917	20/03/1917
War Diary	Caix E.3 Rosieres Sheet	20/03/1917	30/03/1917
War Diary	Nesle I.19 Sheet 66 D.	31/03/1917	31/03/1917
Heading	War Diary of 35 D.A.C. from April 1-April 30th 1917. (Volume 15).		
War Diary	Nesle I.19 Sheet 66 D.	01/04/1917	11/04/1917
War Diary	Monchy-Lagache V.18 Central Sheet 62C	11/04/1917	13/04/1917
War Diary	Monchy-Lagache I.19 Sheet 66 D	14/04/1917	30/04/1917
Heading	War Diary of 35th D.A.C from May 1st-May 31st 1917. (Volume 16).		
War Diary	Monchy Lagache V.18 Cent. Sheet 62 C	01/05/1917	22/05/1917
War Diary	Doingt I.36 Sheet 62c	23/05/1917	24/05/1917
War Diary	Nurlu D.16.a 62c	25/05/1917	31/05/1917
Heading	War Diary of 35 D.A.C. from June 1st June 31st 1917. Vol 17		
War Diary	Nurlu D.16.a 62 C.	01/06/1917	30/06/1917
Heading	War Diary of 35 D.A.C From July 1st to July 31st 1917. (Volume 18).		
War Diary	Nurlu D.16.a 62.C.	01/07/1917	06/07/1917
War Diary	K.13.b 62.c	07/07/1917	09/07/1917
War Diary	Hamel K.13.b 62.C	10/07/1917	31/07/1917
Heading	War Diary of 35th D.A.C from 1st 31st August 1917. (Volume 19).		
War Diary	Marquaix K.13.b Sheet 62.C	01/08/1917	26/08/1917

War Diary	Lieramont D.12.d Sheet 62.C.	27/08/1917	31/08/1917
Heading	War Diary of 35th D.A.C from 1st-30th September 1917. (Volume 20).		
War Diary	Lieramont D.12.d Sheet 62.C	01/09/1917	30/09/1917
Heading	War Diary of 35th D.A.C. from 1st-31st October 1917. (Volume 21).		
War Diary	Lieramont D.12.d 62.C.	01/10/1917	03/10/1917
War Diary	Buire J.32.a. 62.C.	04/10/1917	15/10/1917
War Diary	Near Elverdinghe B.16.a. Sheet 28	16/10/1917	19/10/1917
War Diary	Near Elverdinghe B.16.a	20/10/1917	22/10/1917
War Diary	Near Elverdinghe B.13.a	23/10/1917	31/10/1917
Heading	War Diary of 35th D.A.C. from 1st-30th November 1917. (Volume 22).		
War Diary	Near Elverdinghe B.13.a	01/11/1917	30/11/1917
Heading	35th Division Ammunition Column from 1st December 1917 to 31st December 1917. Volume 23		
War Diary	Near Elverdinghe B.13.a Sheet 27	01/12/1917	09/12/1917
War Diary	E.10.d.7.8 Sheet 27	10/12/1917	12/12/1917
War Diary	Arneke Area H.18.c Central Sheet 27	13/12/1917	31/12/1917
Heading	35th Division Ammunition Column from 1st January 1918. to 31st January 1918. Volume 24		
War Diary	Arneke H.18.c.4.6 Sheet 27	01/01/1918	10/01/1918
War Diary	Handhoek F.24.a.9. & F.14.c.8.6	11/01/1918	14/01/1918
War Diary	Elverdinghe B.13.a.3.7 Sheet 28	15/01/1918	31/01/1918
Heading	35th Division Ammunition Column from 1st February 1918 to 28 February 1918. Volume 25		
War Diary	Elverdinghe Belgium Map Sheet 28-B.13.a.3.7. Rousseel Farm.	01/02/1918	28/02/1918
Miscellaneous	Articles Salvaged Between 15/1/18 and 28/2/18	15/01/1918	15/01/1918
Heading	35th Divisional Ammunition Column from 1st April 1918 to 30 April 1918. Volume 27		
War Diary	Sheet 62D B.30.a.x.c.	01/04/1918	01/04/1918
War Diary	Sheet 62 D. H.18.a.	02/04/1918	03/04/1918
War Diary	Pont Noyelles	04/04/1918	09/04/1918
War Diary	Pont Noyelles Sheet 62 D H.18.a	10/04/1918	12/04/1918
War Diary	Sheet 57 D V.2.a.b.x.c.	12/04/1918	12/04/1918
War Diary	Toutencourt	13/04/1918	14/04/1918
War Diary	Sheet 57 D V.2.a.b.c.	15/04/1918	15/04/1918
War Diary	Toutencourt	16/04/1918	22/04/1918
War Diary	Sheet 57 D, V.2.a.b. & c Toutencourt.	23/04/1918	30/04/1918
Heading	35th Divisional Ammunition Column from 1st May 1918 to 31st May 1918. Volume 28		
War Diary	Toutencourt Sheet 57D. V.2.a	01/05/1918	31/05/1918
Heading	35th Divisional Ammunition Column from 1st June 1918 to 30 June 1918. Volume 29		
War Diary	Toutencourt Sheet 57D. V.2.a	01/06/1918	16/06/1918
War Diary	O.25.c.9.7. Sheet 57 D	17/06/1918	17/06/1918
War Diary	Bois Creftel O.25.d.7.6. Sheet 57 D.	18/06/1918	30/06/1918
Heading	35th Divisional Ammunition Column. from 1st July 1918 to 31st July 1918. Volume 30		
War Diary	Bois Creftel O.25.d.7.6. Sheet 57 D.	01/07/1918	01/07/1918
War Diary	Sheet 27. Oudezeele I.18.b.1.6	02/07/1918	03/07/1918
War Diary	Sheet 27. Steenvoorde Q.1.c.2.5	04/07/1918	04/07/1918
War Diary	Pansgat Fme	05/07/1918	08/07/1918
War Diary	Sheet 27 Pansgat Fme Q.1.c.2.5	09/07/1918	31/07/1918

Heading	35th Divisional Ammunition Column from 1st August 1918 to 31st August 1918. Volume 31		
War Diary	Sheet 27 Q.1.c.2.5. Pamsgat Fme.	01/08/1918	31/08/1918
Heading	35th Divisional Ammunition Column from 1st September 1918 to 30th September 1918. Volume 32		
War Diary	Sheet 27 Q.1.c.2.5. Pamsgat Farm	01/09/1918	01/09/1918
War Diary	Sheet 27 E.17.b.9.7. Pontypool Camp	02/09/1918	02/09/1918
War Diary	Hamhoek A.25.b.1.9	03/09/1918	07/09/1918
War Diary	Eikhoek F.2.8.b.7.2. Sheet 27	08/09/1918	15/09/1918
War Diary	Zwynland Brewery L. 11. d. 9.7. Sheet 27	16/09/1918	16/09/1918
War Diary	Sheet 27 Z.18.a.8.7	17/09/1918	26/09/1918
War Diary	Sheet 28 Moose Jaw Farm H.8.c.6.2	27/09/1918	30/09/1918
Heading	35th Divisional Ammunition Column R.F.A. from. 1st October 1918 to 31st October 1918. Volume 33		
War Diary	Sheet 28 Transport Farm I.2.a.5.2	01/10/1918	13/10/1918
War Diary	Sheet 28 J.2.9.a.5.5. Gheluvelt	14/10/1918	16/10/1918
War Diary	Sheet 28 K.2.2.b.5.8. Peutevin Wood	17/10/1918	20/10/1918
War Diary	Sheet 29 G.3.5.a. Bisseghem	21/10/1918	27/10/1918
War Diary	Sheet 29 O.9.c.2.5	28/10/1918	31/10/1918
Heading	35th Divisional Ammunition Column from 1st November 1918 to 30th November 1918. Volume 34		
War Diary	Sheet 29 O.9.c.2.5	01/11/1918	02/11/1918
War Diary	Courtrai Sheet 29 H.3.2.d.6.8	03/11/1918	05/11/1918
War Diary	Sheet 29 O.3. Central	06/11/1918	10/11/1918
War Diary	Molenhoek Sheet 29 P.3.0.a.6.9	11/11/1918	17/11/1918
War Diary	Cuerne Sheet 29 H.9.b.6.4	18/11/1918	30/11/1918
Heading	35th Divisional Ammunition Column Royal Field Artillery from 1st December 1918 to 31st December 1918. Volume 35		
War Diary	The Collage Menin	01/12/1918	01/12/1918
War Diary	Brown Camp Sheet 28 A.22.d.9.4	02/12/1918	02/12/1918
War Diary	Terdeghem Sheet 27 P.10. Central	03/12/1918	03/12/1918
War Diary	Nieurlet Sheet 27 M.14. a.	04/12/1918	31/12/1918
Heading	35th Divisional Ammunition Column Royal Field Artillery from 1st January 1919 to 31st January 1919. Volume 36		
War Diary	Nieurlet Sheet 27 M.14.a.	01/01/1919	31/01/1919
Heading	35 Divisional Ammunition Column Royal Field Artillery from 1st February 1919 to 28 February 1919. Volume 37		
War Diary	Nieurlet	01/02/1919	28/02/1919
Miscellaneous	35 D.A.	01/04/1919	01/04/1919
Heading	35 Division Ammunition Column Royal Field Artillery from 1st March 1919 to 31st March 1919. Volume 38		
War Diary	Nieurlet Sheet 27 M.14.a	01/03/1919	31/03/1919
Heading	War Diary 35th Divisional Ammunition Column, R.F.A. March 1916		
Heading	35th Divisional Ammunition Column from 1st March 1918 to 31st March 1918. Volume 26		
War Diary	Elverdinghe Belgium Map Sheet 28 B.13.a.3.7. Rousseel Farm.	01/03/1918	23/03/1918
War Diary	Sheet 62 D L.25.a.	24/03/1918	24/03/1918
War Diary	Sheet 62 D Q.4.a	25/03/1918	25/03/1918
War Diary	Sheet 57 D V.25.a	26/03/1918	29/03/1918
War Diary	Sheet 62 D. B.30.a & c.	30/03/1918	31/03/1918

WO95/2475
35 Div
Jan '16 - Mar '19
Div. Ammunition Column

(3)

35TH DIVISION
DIVL ARTILLERY

35TH DIVL AMMN COLUMN

JAN 1916 - MAR 1919

35TH DIVISION
DIVL ARTILLERY

WAR DIARY
INTELLIGENCE SUMMARY.

Army Form C. 2118.

35 D.A.C.

Hour, Date, Place	Summary of Events and Information	Remarks and references to Appendices
Noon 28th Jan 1916 Bedford Camp	Ordered overseas, ordered to embark at Southampton on the 1st Feb 1916, taking the rear of the 35th Div. Artillery.	
29th & 30th Jan. 1916.	Packing up and drawing stores to bring Unit up to Establishment.	
31st Jan - 1st Feby	Starting from 3 am. Column was entrained at AMESBURY in 8 different parties each comprising roughly 114 MEN 14 VEHICLES and 68 horses an interval of two hours between parties from Camp, and one hour between departure of trains most train parties were completely entrained at least 15 minutes before the schedule time and in all cases considering the men were quite new to entrainments done very well. The last party departed from AMESBURY at 1.35 pm. this comprised mostly 14 Staff and part of a Section. On arrival at Southampton which was roughly about 3.30 pm embarkation Officers had taken command of trains as they arrived and embarked parties on to the various transports then available. The system was very good and takes a very great weight off OC. On his arrival he may find out quite easily what has become of his command in a very short space of time.	

O H Parr Major
OC

Army Form C. 2118.

WAR DIARY
or
INTELLIGENCE SUMMARY. 35 D.A.C.

(Erase heading not required.)

Army Form C. 2118.   II

Hour, Date, Place	Summary of Events and Information	Remarks and references to Appendices
1st Feb 1916.	By the time I arrived the majority had left, and the balance embarked and left on the Transport. MADRAS. A large and comfortable boat. Our strength on board was 130 MEN 140 horses and MULES. 100men and above this amount were 1 Battery complete and Bde Ammunition Column, belonging to 15gth Bde R.F.A. We sailed at 7.45 P.M. weather smooth and my instructions were when we picked up the Escort that all lights were to be extinguished, at about 10 P.M. this was done but I was not informed whether Escort was there or not, life belts were served out to every man on board and Officers detailed to examine same where put on. Horses were accommodated all the way round the ship and were watered and fed twice during the voyage. On arrival at disembarkation wharf no casualties were reported. We arrived alongside about 9 a.m. & disem- barkation began about immediately. The M.L.O. informed me we were to be billeted in Hut 3, & the wagons were to be parked about ½ mile distant	
2nd Feb. Hare		

WAR DIARY
or
~~INTELLIGENCE~~ SUMMARY. 35 D.O.C.

(Erase heading not required.)

Army Form C. 2118.

III

Instructions regarding War Diaries and Intelligence Summaries are contained in F.S. Regs., Part II and the Staff Manual respectively. Title pages will be prepared in manuscript.

Hour, Date, Place	Summary of Events and Information	Remarks and references to Appendices
Havre Feb 2. 1916	~~advice~~ near the River Ship containing the German prisoners. The parking of the vehicles after disembarkation was completed by about 2.30 when the men had their dinners. Received orders to entrain Thursday 3rd Feb.	
Feb. 3.	2/3 coy Nos 1 and 2 sections entrained at Point 1 during the evening.	
Feb 4	2/3 coy No 3 section entrained in morning at Point 1. Remaining 1/3 of Nos 2 & 3 section entrained Feb evening at Point 1. Remaining 1/3 of Nos section & headquarters entrained at Point 3 at 5 A.M. The whole column occupied in all 5 trains each train carrying approx of 114 officers and men and 23 vehicles. Detrainment	
Feb 5	over 150 horses and no men lefted. Mules were quite unruly & no horse affected. The new method of trucking. The CO long & difficult piece of work. Horses were not as much shaken	A.D.V.S. HAV S/1/a

WAR DIARY or INTELLIGENCE SUMMARY.

Army Form C. 2118.

35 J.A.C.

(Erase heading not required.)

Hour, Date, Place	Summary of Events and Information	Remarks and references to Appendices
Feb 5. 1916	Spent the whole day in the train.	
Feb 6. Arques	Arrived at Wizernes at 1.30 a.m. Detraining started immediately. Marched to Arques & arrived there at 7.30. Headquarters billeted in a Brewery. Refectors near Hon. Coulur in Archange. Maj. Ferrey called. Reg. for Stanley called in the morning & as I was absent long gone to H.Q. at Wallephem, he came back again in the afternoon. Lt. Cassidy R.A.M.C. attached.	
Feb 8	Capt. Lee R.A.M.C. took Lieut Cassidy's duty. Received orders to move to Renescure known 9th. Sent Adjutant & Interpreter to reconnoitre	

WAR DIARY
or
INTELLIGENCE SUMMARY.

(Erase heading not required.)

Army Form C. 2118.

35 F.A.C.

Hour, Date, Place	Summary of Events and Information	Remarks and references to Appendices
Aques Feb 9. 1916	Marched from Aques at 8.15. My orders were to be clear of Meurinsten at 10.20 & not to enter Aqnes until the 157th Regiment had cleared it. We were clear of Meuringhen at 10.10 & head of column reached where Regiment was found to be in at 10.20. The 157 Regt was found to be in Aqnes. We were delayed outside Aqnes for about 1 hour 45 minutes on account of the 157 Regt not being able to follow as they were held up by another Brigade. We then Arrived at Hamety at 1.30. The column arrived as I was not satisfied with the te le purphon interview with Major reported	[signature]
Hamety		

(73989) W4141—463. 400,000. 9/14. H.&J.Ltd. Forms/C. 2118/10.

Army Form C. 2118.

WAR DIARY
or
INTELLIGENCE SUMMARY. 35 T.Q.C.

(Erase heading not required.)

Instructions regarding War Diaries and Intelligence Summaries are contained in F.S. Regs., Part II. and the Staff Manual respectively. Title pages will be prepared in manuscript.

Hour, Date, Place	Summary of Events and Information	Remarks and references to Appendices
Hunts, Feb 9. 1916	horse changes, & decided to see him myself. Found her finally & very shortspoken. Had great difficulties, & had to accommodate trooper horses in sheds. Moved into Hunts at 3.30. He had their canvas immediately.	
Feb 10-	No change. Received orders late that [line] would be received next day by Lord Rebecca. His & place later noticed later.	
Feb 11-	Received orders at 2 a.m. convoy Rammel. Paraded at 6.30 a.m. marched off to meet Sir Ian at Kenalis. Found [?] ordered one. Arrived at Redgrove at 10 a.m.	

WAR DIARY or INTELLIGENCE SUMMARY

Army Form C. 2118.

35 D.Q.C

VII

Hour, Date, Place	Summary of Events and Information	Remarks and references to Appendices
Friday Feb 11. 1916	Returned to Billets at 1.45 P.M. from very cold trek. C.O. conference at Parkes at 4.30 P.M.	
Feb 12"-	Lectured Coys. No change. Relieved with Jap on Revr. Dumples, Academy etc.	
Feb 13"-	Instituted competition between Kent & the Planters Church Forres at Repair. 6.30 P.M.	
Feb 14"-	No change. Revd for Staveley called.	
Feb 15	No change. Gen Staveley called and went round those bits of No 2 Section and to Blockhouse. Competition held in afternoon & not all of Lammas.	J.M.Clark Maj.

Army Form C. 2118.

WAR DIARY
or
INTELLIGENCE SUMMARY. 35 D.A.C.

(Erase heading not required.)

VIII

Instructions regarding War Diaries and Intelligence Summaries are contained in F.S. Regs., Part II. and the Staff Manual respectively. Title pages will be prepared in manuscript.

Hour, Date, Place	Summary of Events and Information	Remarks and references to Appendices

Namely Feb 15 1916 — Work by No 1 Echelon. Rent completed down at the dump and am by No 3 Echelon to the 163 Bde both. Received orders to fill up 163 Bde with 2336 rounds H.S. (4.5 How) & 160 Shrapnel & 270 H.E. (18 pdr) Ammunition together 2000 rounds S.A.A. which is to be Park. Then in place 2400. 18 pdr H.E. Lent 800 rounds of this to each Bde 157. 152. 159. together from their own ammunition reserve 18pdr Shrapnel which is to be returned.

Worked all night completed 163 Bde 9.5" Ammunition. Kept one spare

(Sgd) W. Roy Major O.C.

(73989) W4141—463. 400,000. 9/14. H.&J. Ltd. Forms/C. 2118/10.

Army Form C. 2118.

WAR DIARY
or
INTELLIGENCE SUMMARY.   35 D.A.C.   IX

(Erase heading not required.)

Hour, Date, Place	Summary of Events and Information	Remarks and references to Appendices
Monday Feb. 16	Started north of LaPark linents to load up reserve. Worked all day loading Ammunition. 10 p.m. No change. Received two rounds 18/pr in our waggons.	
Feb 17.	Stopped for Repairs & packed kens. No effect of Colour attested Audit for Refuge at Hazlles. Received head roll also one P.M. F. Divisional arms Column 19th arts.	O/Parker Mjr RFA

WAR DIARY
or
INTELLIGENCE SUMMARY.

Army Form C. 2118.

35 T.A.C.

(Erase heading not required.)

Instructions regarding War Diaries and Intelligence Summaries are contained in F.S. Regs., Part II and the Staff Manual respectively. Title pages will be prepared in manuscript.

Hour, Date, Place	Summary of Events and Information	Remarks and references to Appendices
Ruff. Feb 18th	Salage. C.R.A. called & enquired of we expected of hard ammunition line. Shyped at one report & then repeated 10pr 15-9 + 4.5 H.P. answered.	
Feb 19. Frame 6 - Kawacheyne	Column passing up observation line. Packed at A.40 A.R. Column to start at Wire - line lost 11.30 a.m. then at Column arrived halt at 10.15 to from 157 Column arrived here but 1 Cool Rocky Reports coming from Festum alcard to 4.30 10.45 has Festum alcard from Darel at 11.0 Column not chages	

WAR DIARY
INTELLIGENCE SUMMARY. 35 D.A.C.

Army Form C. 2118. XL

Hour, Date, Place	Summary of Events and Information	Remarks and references to Appendices
March Havrincourt Feb 19	Division at 11.30. Took over line from 12.30 to 1st Def. from offensive about 12.30. Arrived at Havrincourt at 2.30. Rain. Clear. Relieved clearing party at wood in company cookers. Men had their dinners about 4. 30 P.M. Here advised that Remd. crossed at I.B.E. Epehy in moving dept of b'talns but meet to cycle away to all ranks. Batallions became. Coys.A Cook Males I Lg. Cooks trained Cos I M. Guns Whole Gunners Nos 1 and 3 mays from Gunl. the	
Feb 20		

O.M.P. Reiley Maj
D.A.A.

WAR DIARY
or
INTELLIGENCE SUMMARY.

(Erase heading not required.)

Army Form C. 2118.

35 T.A.C.

XII

Hour, Date, Place	Summary of Events and Information	Remarks and references to Appendices
Hennencourt 20/2/16	And refresh wheels.	
Feb 21. 1916	Tested R.W.T. Recd. message at 10.45 a.m. to prepare for attack. Later — Recd. orders at 7.23 P.M. to send 10 wagons only with further orders to follow later. R.O. taken today with standings. Other sections have no trick. Section Commanders & R.O. attended lecture at Hénencourt on Ammunition returns. Ammunition and marks on boxes.	[signature]

WAR DIARY
or
INTELLIGENCE SUMMARY. 35 D.A.C.

Army Form C. 2118.
XII

(Erase heading not required.)

Hour, Date, Place	Summary of Events and Information	Remarks and references to Appendices
Haverskerque Feb 21	Gen Penny called in the afternoon.	
Feb 22	No change	
Feb 23	Rec'd 1250 shells and fuzes. Sent to N9 Bde Ingoytan. 250 to N7 Bde Ingoytan. No change. Gen Lawton called & inspected lines.	
Feb 24	No change. Rec'd 5760 rifle cart. Gunner Ledford 108th L Batty Bde reported sick & died immediately in reply to Doctor query.	O.C. Asst Mjr A.A. O.C Asst Mjr A.A.

WAR DIARY
or
INTELLIGENCE SUMMARY
(Erase heading not required.)

Army Form C. 2118.

35 F.A.O.

XIV

Instructions regarding War Diaries and Intelligence Summaries are contained in F.S. Regs., Part II. and the Staff Manual respectively. Title pages will be prepared in manuscript.

Hour, Date, Place	Summary of Events and Information	Remarks and references to Appendices
Hazenbrouck Feb 26. 1916	In charge. Today Recvd orders to report to Section 1. O. 16. g. 22 (French) area also to 20th F.A.O. whose information refers to 20 F.A.O. whose field is on Ap360	
Feb 27	Ordered to No 1 Sektor to are c 2/3/16 16. g 22. 20 F.A.O. has to inform 35th F.A.O. For purpose reckon F on 16 35 F.A.O. R is ordered to report to 16 35 F.A.O. Rest Cat 157 of O. g. 6.62 + report. Sent cat 157 20 F.A.O. 24 F.A. Refer to g of p 360.	M. Bury M—O.H. M. Bury M—O.H.

Army Form C. 2118.

WAR DIARY
or
INTELLIGENCE SUMMARY.

35 S.A.A.

(Erase heading not required.)

Hour, Date, Place	Summary of Events and Information	Remarks and references to Appendices
Mauerguergue Feb 28th 1916	Archange. Arr. of No 1 Section to Guenchin carried out. Arranged for section to take up supply of ammunition at 12 midnight.	
Feb 29th	Archange. German Biplane brought down near Los Section at G. 10 d 5.2. Map 36 A. Pilot wounded Observer uninjured. Machine practically intact except for propeller.	A.B. Ackerman Major

35th D.A.C.
Supplement to
Vol. I

Supplementary to War Diary
for February.

Army Form C. 2118.

35th F.A.C.

WAR DIARY
or
INTELLIGENCE SUMMARY.
(Erase heading not required.)

Instructions regarding War Diaries and Intelligence Summaries are contained in F.S. Regs., Part II. and the Staff Manual respectively. Title pages will be prepared in manuscript.

Hour, Date, Place	Summary of Events and Information	Remarks and references to Appendices
List of Officers	Serving on Active Service with 35 F.A.C. 1st February 1915. From Butters.	
Major A.H. Bersey	Commanding	
Lieut B.J. Counah	Adjutant	
Lieut B.M.R. Ingram	O/c No 1 Sec.	
2Lieut J.S. Thompson	"	
" L.A. Brook	"	
Capt A. Smith	O/c No 2 Sec.	
Lieut P.J. Scott	"	
Capt E. Clonqui Birrell	O/c No 3 Sec.	
Lieut A. Vore	"	
2Lieut R.A. Scott	"	

35th D.A.G.
Vol I

35 T.A.C. North of Arras

WAR DIARY
or
INTELLIGENCE SUMMARY.

Army Form C. 2118.

Hour, Date, Place	Summary of Events and Information	Remarks and references to Appendices
Havrincourt March 1.3.1916	Nothing fresh to report	35 Div A cdt Vol 2
2	ditto	
3	ditto	
4	ditto	
5	Nothing fresh. German aeroplane dropped bombs near Watch Post. No 3 taken Re	
6	Garage done. Nothing fresh	
7	ditto	
8	Received orders to move to H. Floris, to clear of billets by 12 and taken Inspect	

Army Form C. 2118.

WAR DIARY
or
INTELLIGENCE SUMMARY.
(Erase heading not required.)

March

Instructions regarding War Diaries and Intelligence Summaries are contained in F. S. Regs., Part II. and the Staff Manual respectively. Title pages will be prepared in manuscript.

Hour, Date, Place	Summary of Events and Information	Remarks and references to Appendices
Mazingarbe 8/3/16	enhearse to St Vaast before 11 o'clock. G.O.C. R.A. called in afternoon to test conference of R.O (O.C.) at I.A.H.Q.	
St Floris 9/3/16	Proud to St Floris distance about 3 kilometers at 10.30 convoy [horse?] about 11.20. No. 3 Section which badly in the [mud?] in the field where wagons had been parked at T.21.C. It took hours from 6 a.m. to about 11.30 to get wagons out. Every wagon had to be unloaded, & the whole section turned on to pull them out with drag ropes. The Co. [?] [?] put up to the [?] [?]	

WAR DIARY or INTELLIGENCE SUMMARY

Army Form C. 2118.

March

(Erase heading not required.)

Hour, Date, Place	Summary of Events and Information	Remarks and references to Appendices
En Gloris 9/3/16	This was the only field, or rather the best field obtainable. The action however was already one map of the enemy's scheme of the ground. However had done to support the troops which simply disappeared into the air when under to the river little. Never seen to the action from Gr. 16. 2. 2. T Recalled to 1 Section in its place. Sent to 3 Section forward in its place. Observed artillery to front.	
10/3/16	Sent forward 6 wagons to C.R.8 at 2 o'clock. 1 permanent fatigues. In addition we supplied 9 others for other fatigues.	
11/3/16		
12/3/16	Received orders to send forward 1 Ambulance & 2 G.S. Wagons to the advanced section. These	O/C Amb. [signature]

Army Form C. 2118.

WAR DIARY
or
INTELLIGENCE SUMMARY.   March

(Erase heading not required.)

Instructions regarding War Diaries and Intelligence Summaries are contained in F.S. Regs., Part II. and the Staff Manual respectively. Title pages will be prepared in manuscript.

Hour, Date, Place	Summary of Events and Information	Remarks and references to Appendices
Le Florie 12/3/16	were supplied by No 2 Section.	
13/3/16	Lothing fresh. Lack of officers available to Lt Renault Lowed hisher relief to learn all they could about Bomb Store Bombs & Marks.	
14/3/16	No change. Inspection of Renault crossed by Major Gibson improvement.	
15/3/16	No change. Inspector Lavers of avenue section at Gerchi. Left quick sub depot & deceed to hand to Capt Crossall for command of No 3 Section honoured for	[signature]

WAR DIARY
or
INTELLIGENCE SUMMARY.

Army Form C. 2118.

(Erase heading not required.)

March

Hour, Date, Place	Summary of Events and Information	Remarks and references to Appendices
St Floris 16/3/16	Ordered No 3 Section together from Grenke to St Floris, & No 2 Section to take the place. Capt Crowe's party returned to St Floris. Recent work began in place. 1st Lieut Goul Hampford to No 2 Sec 2nd Lieut Slaven " " No 1 to No 2, to No 3 2nd Lt Thompson " " No 1 to No 3. 2nd Lt Bott to command No 3. Alleged Turks Don't demonstrate at Neuve Chapelle, took all officers that could be spared.	

WAR DIARY
or
INTELLIGENCE SUMMARY.

(Erase heading not required.)

Army Form C. 2118.

Month: March 1916

Hour, Date, Place	Summary of Events and Information	Remarks and references to Appendices
St Floris 17/3/16	Lochops inspected No 2 section at Grewte in their new filets	
18/3/16	Lochops. Horses inspection No 1 & No 3 section. Weather improving. very fine. O.C. No 3 section returned from short leave to England. C.R.A. called on enemy	
19/3/16	Lochops Church Parade 2.30. Received orders on telephone from 38th Batt Rd Artillery this at 8 sevens used but to take to Lochpost	

WAR DIARY
or
INTELLIGENCE SUMMARY. March

(Erase heading not required.)

Army Form C. 2118.

Hour, Date, Place	Summary of Events and Information	Remarks and references to Appendices
St Eloi 20/3/16	No change. Received orders to move to Havrincourt tomorrow 21/3/16. Adjt Capt. called & stated we are one at our own time. Received orders to dump immediately 50 18pr shrapnel and 25 18pr H.E. making 25 rounds per 18pr gun and 5 Shrapnel & 35 H.E. per 4.5 Howitzer, making 40 rounds per 4.5 Howitzer. Above dumped at ful road G.11.c.6.2. where 1200 18pr Shrapnel & 600 18pr H.E. were dumped during night & that 400 rounds to dumped at the	[signature]

WAR DIARY
or
INTELLIGENCE SUMMARY.

Army Form C. 2118.

Month: March

Hour, Date, Place	Summary of Events and Information	Remarks and references to Appendices
St. Floris 20/3/16	Hopkins at Haverskerque at T.27.a.6.5. stopped A.S.C. lorries which were out to obtain from Renescure, & therefore H.Q. was drawn a blank. The 157 Rds already had 296 loads on them. Checked in excess of establishment on hand. Therefore this had to be taken into consideration. Total amount dumped at Haverskerque, was 157 H.Q. therefore Oats 157 lb. Hay, Oats 640 A.S.H.Q.	
21/3/16	Foregoing dump was completed by 5·30 P.M. Moved to Haverskerque R.H.Q. hr.	

Army Form C. 2118.

WAR DIARY
or
INTELLIGENCE SUMMARY. Reich

(Erase heading not required.)

Instructions regarding War Diaries and Intelligence Summaries are contained in F. S. Regs., Part II. and the Staff Manual respectively. Title pages will be prepared in manuscript.

Hour, Date, Place	Summary of Events and Information	Remarks and references to Appendices
Mavenkerque 21/3/16	No 3 Section occupying Fillebet at P.8.6.4.7 No 1 Section occupying Pillbox at T.21.c.10.2 and T.21.c.6.2. Received orders from O.R.A. to proceed to O.C. 33rd D.A.C. at G.3.a.5.9. to receive from him details as to Kemmetete required for dumps & O.P. materials. When the dumps moves.	
22/3/16	Received order cancelling above totally that intent of above move to 33 Div. Ark was postponed. No change	

WAR DIARY
or
INTELLIGENCE SUMMARY.   March

(Erase heading not required.)

Army Form C. 2118.

Hour, Date, Place	Summary of Events and Information	Remarks and references to Appendices
Mavrobergun 24/3/16	Received orders that Levien brigade were to our area, where our pt. 2nd Inf. Bn. gave. Sent orders as to date of checkation of this unit.	
25/3/16	Heavy rain over our area would be Sorbier. Rode over there. Saw Col. Beaudrie comm'g. 9th D.A.C. Arranged about Adjutant our next day to see Rillet, rekadersch.	
26/3/16	Rochaye. Adjutant went to Sorbier.	
27/3/16	Ditto	
28/3/16	Ditto. Adjutant went over to Sorbier with no 1 Coy. Capt. Cockerion in command of same & no 2 R.C.O. to take over billets.	O.C. early hr.

WAR DIARY
or
INTELLIGENCE SUMMARY. March

(Erase heading not required.)

Army Form C. 2118.

Hour, Date, Place	Summary of Events and Information	Remarks and references to Appendices
Havrincourt 29/3/16	No change. Received orders at 9.45 P.M. K.5 area to ours Area namely Jonlieu, watching alarm ours teure. Following orders issued W.G. to move so as to be clear of K.25.d.5.58 at 1 P.M. to halt. No. 1 Bn. to move so as to be clear of Jonlieu Sqdrs T.30.d.7.0. at 1.15 P.M. & halt. No.3 Bn. to move so that head of recce could reach Jonlieu crossroads T.30.d.7.0. at 1.15 P.M. & halt. Column then to move in following order No.1 Recce No.3 W.G. Convoy followed by No.1 Recce, bringing up the rear. No.2 Recce will move so that head of recce	XI

Army Form C. 2118.

WAR DIARY
or
INTELLIGENCE SUMMARY.   March XII

(Erase heading not required.)

Instructions regarding War Diaries and Intelligence Summaries are contained in F.S. Regs., Part II. and the Staff Manual respectively. Title pages will be prepared in manuscript.

Hour, Date, Place	Summary of Events and Information	Remarks and references to Appendices
Havrincourt 29/3/16 30/3/16	will reach Q. 13. 6. 9.0 at 2.45 P.M. & halt & finally bad column into any likely area. We were however out to listen & the march was very disheartening enough, the to 2 keehin away from Grenche Q. 16. 22. Map 36A were not allowed to take the road elected & therefore had to march in rear of No.3 instead of leading column. C. R. A. arrived at Sorleen as column came in. G.O.C. 30th Div. called Kempster to 1 and 2 Seehino.	[signature]
Sorleen 31/3/16		

Army Form C. 2118.

WAR DIARY
or
INTELLIGENCE SUMMARY.
(Erase heading not required.)

352 W
A Col
North of Ypres
Vol 35

Hour, Date, Place	Summary of Events and Information	Remarks and references to Appendices
Poelcap[elle] 1/4/16	2nd Lt Thompson sent to hospital 27/3/16. Capt Gorges resumed command from 1st Apl. Posted to command No. 3 Battery. Received letter from G.O.C Canterbury. B.S.R. on one cent…	
2/4/16	At rest. Large amount of ammunition & other material arrived. New wagon axles & every material etc.	
3/4/16	Wagon inspection held. Issues to 2nd Lt Washington & Lieut 1/5 3 Guns. Return despatched. Kin posted L. 15 3 am. Return despatched for in B.M. & notes that 2nd Lt Johnson was sent to Base to follow on to B S Battery T.C.	
4/4/16	At the first change Captain Bergeaud still Chief of change. Compiled C.O.S inspected wagons.	
5/4/16	No change.	

WAR DIARY or INTELLIGENCE SUMMARY

Army Form C. 2118.

II

April

(Erase heading not required.)

Hour, Date, Place	Summary of Events and Information	Remarks and references to Appendices
Lonleur 7/4/16	No change. Called at R.A. Headquarters at Tailly.	
8/4/16	No change. Called at R.A. H.Q. Saw C.R.A. & obtained leave for him to an officer from a rifle section/identity squadron.	
9/4/16	No change. Horses of 4th Division arriving 12 wagons carrying 760 ready shells. A.S. 37 Frenies 13 Runners 3 cars over. Reconnd of Kent. Liffect Pickerick.	
10/4/16	A.S.M.T. called. Visited R.A. HQ. a afternoon. Officers no change.	
11/4/16	No change. Visited XI Corps Amm. Park.	

WAR DIARY or INTELLIGENCE SUMMARY

Army Form C. 2118.

Hour, Date, Place	Summary of Events and Information	Remarks and references to Appendices
Harleen 12/4/16	No change.	
13/4/16	Rec'd. 38 Ser. M.G. + R.A.M.C. Rep. told he should one to remain, the other at quant. No change. Ration to Greenhill Camp also killed. Found it over he informed Capt. ??? that area needed into that area Reports sent.	
14/4/16	No change. Held examination of J.C. ??? Machine Ammunition. Adjutant ordered Keys to R.A.M.C. to see about new new battery, namely Paradio.	
15/4/16	No change. Adjutant took over to Paradio. O. 18 A.C. Rethene conferred officer + retted Billets. Received orders we were to move Monday 17th inst. to Ecolin Knolen Donloi. (signature)	

Army Form C. 2118.

WAR DIARY
or
INTELLIGENCE SUMMARY.
(Erase heading not required.)

April IV

Instructions regarding War Diaries and Intelligence Summaries are contained in F.S. Regs., Part II. and the Staff Manual respectively. Title pages will be prepared in manuscript.

Hour, Date, Place	Summary of Events and Information	Remarks and references to Appendices
Julien 15/4/16	by 8 a.m. 1 section horsemen behind not made till relieved by Anglesea S.A.O. 2 Lt Bentison to 2nd Ambulance	
16/4/16	Recharge. Afghabat section open to Reads but Lebie Officers to effect this killed. Reported some occupied by infantry killed.	
Joulien - Paradis 17/4/16	Column moved to Paradis G. 18. a.e. a. Ford filled occupied by infantry ordered. Arranged to double up for one night Infantry moved out & Column moved into Ras Hilila	
18/4/16		
19/4/16	No change. Held conference Lut-Col Commandant (W Berly Mar) and decided to start Reports to Carleen	

(73969) W4141—463. 400,000. 9/14. H.&J.Ltd. Forms/C. 2118/10.

WAR DIARY
or
INTELLIGENCE SUMMARY.

Army Form C. 2118.

April

(Erase heading not required.)

Hour, Date, Place	Summary of Events and Information	Remarks and references to Appendices
Paradis		
19/4/16	Re sale of Tobacco etc.	
20/4/16	Re charge of Sgt Carly authority went to Col Cates from notified by post	
21/4/16	Re charge	
22/4/16	Re charge Vexated R.A. H.Q. at once	
	Vere C.R.A. re Ammunition	
23/4/16	Re charge. Recved letter of Apl 2nd at Thorpen hampered to Sgt cool	
24/4/16	Re charge. Gun Camp Team competition. C.R.A.	
25/4/16	Checked reported shortage of coal. 2nd C.B. Peck attached to Athens Camp 2nd Lankashire unit Lt Col Stewart R.H.A.	

Army Form C. 2118.

WAR DIARY
or
INTELLIGENCE SUMMARY.

(Erase heading not required.)

Instructions regarding War Diaries and Intelligence Summaries are contained in F.S. Regs., Part II. and the Staff Manual respectively. Title pages will be prepared in manuscript.

Month: April

Hour, Date, Place	Summary of Events and Information	Remarks and references to Appendices
Paradis 26/4/16	C.R.O. called inspected 24 teams in full marching order knocked peg to No 2 section. 9 Rec Reg reported Trsp. M.G.C. to relieve 1st Feb 5, 1916. Letter GHQ Aff Lg6 cont sub orders Oct/Feb 1188. 27 Lt Rein XI Corps 1188. Command of Kitchen.	
27/4/16 28/4/16	No change. Lecture turret electrician in area of Retter 35.3a. placing no charges. 39'. Major Remington went to Lee depot G.R.Q. respecting leave to be left in G.R.Q to know if you thought leave	MRW 4/9/16

WAR DIARY
or
INTELLIGENCE SUMMARY.
(Erase heading not required.)

Army Form C. 2118.

April

Hour, Date, Place	Summary of Events and Information	Remarks and references to Appendices
Parades 28/4/16	Again picketing wagons to reclaim fire which they were taken.	
29/4/16	Received C.R.A.'s sanction to hook up No 9 section. Lent Helophost Mules to command No 3 Section in place of 2nd Ltd Lewes. In charge C.R.A. collect windpipes. Church Parade.	M Cooke Lt Col

VII

3rd Div. AC

Month of May Vol I

WAR DIARY
or
INTELLIGENCE SUMMARY.

Army Form C. 2118.

(Erase heading not required.)

Instructions regarding War Diaries and Intelligence Summaries are contained in F.S. Regs., Part II. and the Staff Manual respectively. Title pages will be prepared in manuscript.

Hour, Date, Place	Summary of Events and Information	Remarks and references to Appendices
Paradis 1/5/16	No change	
2/5/16	Regular Comy XI Corps inspected Ho. & Co. billets + some of the ammunition wagons inspected full strength over 27 wagons inspected full strength order G.O.C. 3rd Div. inspected Column at 4 P.M. G.S.O.I. inspected horses & mules during the morning	
3/5/16	Horses inspected Ho. & Co.	
4/5/16	No change	
5/5/16	No change	
6/5/16	Received notice 2nd Lt Perrott evacuated to England 20/4/16.	[signature]

WAR DIARY
or
INTELLIGENCE SUMMARY. Month of Mar 19
(Erase heading not required.)

Army Form C. 2118.

Hour, Date, Place	Summary of Events and Information	Remarks and references to Appendices
Paradis 7/5/16 8/5/16	Adjutant went to special leave. Visited R.A. H-Q. was told of new scheme for supply of ammunition, as also of the H-Q. of the J.A.G. as well as the H-Q. of the J.A.G. Reconnoitred new proposed position of H-Q near Lobelia.	
9/5/16	Horses inspected. to 3 Co. Reconnoitred new area reported to R.A. H.Q.	
10/5/16	Horses inspected by Co. Revisited new area reported to R.A. H.Q.	
11/5/16	No change.	[signature]

WAR DIARY
or
INTELLIGENCE SUMMARY. Ray

Army Form C. 2118.

(Erase heading not required.)

Hour, Date, Place	Summary of Events and Information	Remarks and references to Appendices
Ruadie 12/5/16	Lt Thelfall joined & attached to H.Q.	
13/5/16	2nd Lt Hayes joined & posted to 2 Coy	
14/5/16	Rec'd authority to echelon off 2 R.Cs Thirpan plant. D.A.V.S. reports condition of horses etc at this inspection quite satisfactory. H.Q. + No 3 Cables move to 2October	
15/5/16 2 October	Received notice of reorganization. B the R.A.C. + F.A.O. Sal Art. — to be amalgamated, new strength to consist of roughly 880 men 1050 horses 160 vehicles. Held Conference of R.A. com- manders & submitted scheme to R.A. 18 Dr. [signature]	

WAR DIARY or INTELLIGENCE SUMMARY

Army Form C. 2118.

Hour, Date, Place	Summary of Events and Information	Remarks and references to Appendices
2 o'Cloc 15/5/16	Adjutant returned from leave.	
16/5/16	Lt Col Reid went on special leave left 18th	
17/5/16	No change	
18/5/16	Lt Col Reid returned. Conference of R.A.O. commanders re scheme pushed forward. Surplus personnel horses & vehicles to be evacuated to Calais under Capt Crowell on 28th. Remount Depot found at port to fun which _____ deficiencies in establishment.	
19/5/16	Rations carts in the Divn are to be filled up.	

W. R. [signature]

Army Form C. 2118.

WAR DIARY
or
INTELLIGENCE SUMMARY. May
(Erase heading not required.)

Instructions regarding War Diaries and Intelligence Summaries are contained in F.S. Regs., Part II. and the Staff Manual respectively. Title pages will be prepared in manuscript.

Hour, Date, Place	Summary of Events and Information	Remarks and references to Appendices
Lolotes 20/5/16	Recharge, working on scheme	Detail of out-going gun teams attached
21/5/16	Ditto	
22/5/16	Ditto	
23/5/16	Recharge turplus ordered to leave 29/5/16.	
24/5/16	Capt Rowe A.V.C. joined column.	
25/5/16	Received orders suddenly that evacuated party were to leave next morning at 8.a.m	
26/5/16	Party left for Cairo under Capt Rowell with fifteen officers & 24 lieu to Tochin Kapar Wagon Station Road. Heavy rainfall accompanied them. Capt Lowe accompanied them. Lieut Threlfall transferred to M.T. Pte Lieut Threlfall went out to Goll club	

Alfred Lyle

Army Form C. 2118.

WAR DIARY
or
INTELLIGENCE SUMMARY. May

(Erase heading not required.)

VI

Hour, Date, Place	Summary of Events and Information	Remarks and references to Appendices
2 October 27/5/16	No change.	
28/5/16.	Lt Col Ashberry goes on leave. Capt Wilkinson R.F.A. takes over command.	
29/5/16	No change.	
30/5/16.	Bombardment started about 7.30 continued for about 2 hours. Supplied 3376 rounds 10pm to 6.6 4.5 ammunition. Found present dump absolutely inadequate. Officers sent to Calais all absent except Capt Curwel who remained to details.	
31/5/16	2 2nd Lt Jackson sent to hospital. 2 2nd Lieut Potts to 159 Bde & 2nd Lt Hayes & 2nd Lt Johnson Kemp & Pease remain sick. attached to A.P.	[signature]

Sub. Division of Sections I, II + III A Echelon
35th D.A.C.

CAPTAIN
Sergt. Major

1 Grenade Wagon (1380 Grenades)
1 Technical Store Wagon
1 Water Cart
3 Bicycles
2 A.S.C. Wagons attached

Right Section
(16 18pr. Ammn. Wagons)
Senior Subaltern

1 Sergt
1 Corpl

8 18 pr. Wagons
76 rounds each
= 608 rounds

1 Sergt
1 Corpl

8 18 pr. Wagons
76 rounds each
= 608 rounds

= 1216 rounds 18 pr.

Left Section
5. 4.5" How. Wagons
Junior Subaltern

1 Sergt
1 Corpl

5 4.5" How. Wagon
48 rounds each
TOTAL = 240 rds 4.5" How.

3 G.S. Wagons
41 boxes S.A.A. each

1 Sergt
1 Corpl

5 Limber G.S. Wagons
18 boxes S.A.A. each

3 G.S. Wagons
41 boxes S.A.A. each

Total = 336 boxes S.A.A.

5 G.S. 6 4.5
S.A.H.

*NB. Left Section of No II. Section No 6 4.5" How. Wagons with 48 rounds on each = 288 rounds 4.5" How.

Sub-division of Section IV B Echelon

35th D.A.C.

Captain
Sergt. Major

- 1 Grenade Wagon (1380 rounds)
- 1 Technical Store Wagon
- 1 Water Cart
- 1 Wagon G.S. Cooks
- 3 Bicycles
- 4 A.S.C. Wagons attached

Right Section — 2nd in Command — 1 Sgt / 1 Corpl — 1 Sgt / 1 Corpl

Centre Section — Senior Subaltern — 1 Sergt / 1 Corpl — 1 Sergt / 1 Corpl

LEFT SECTION — Junior Subaltern — 1 Sergt / 1 Corpl — 1 Sergt / 1 Corpl

Right Section:
8. 4.5" How. Wagons G.S. — 66 rounds each = 528
8. 18 Pr. G.S. Wagons — 108 rounds each = 864 rounds
8. 4.5" How. Wagons G.S. — 66 rds. each = 528
{ 1056 rounds 4.5" How
  ( ) 18 pr

Centre Section:
4. S.A.A. G.S. Wagon — 42 boxes each = 168
4. 18 pr. G.S. Wagons — 108 rds. each = 432
{ 1296 rounds 18pr
  168 Boxes S.A.A.

Left Section:
8. S.A.A. Wagons G.S. — 42 boxes each = 336
8. S.A.A. Wagons G.S. — 41 boxes each = 328

664 Boxes S.A.A.
Total Boxes S.A.A. in Section = 832

35. D.A.C.
Army Form C. 2118
Vol 5
June

WAR DIARY
or
INTELLIGENCE SUMMARY
(Erase heading not required.)

Place	Date	Hour	Summary of Events and Information	Remarks and references to Appendices
Zeloba	1/6/16		No change	
	2/6		do.	
	3/6		do.	
	4/6		Received warning at 11.10 P.M. of heavy bombardment and heavy gun enemy of own trenches and probably to respond to Messines reduct & stand to. Ammunition ordered for Behah reserve. I.O.H. Fire by opened by Batteries	
	5/6		C.R.O. visited & proposed site for new dump note Adjutant Ordnance.	
	6/6		Lieut Col Peake returned from leave & took over lieut. Fergusons duties.	
	7/6		C.R.A. & Brigade Major came over to look at site for dump	
	8/6		Closed by Col Perly. Copied letter from these workmen	
	9/6		Res. Dumps renewed. Both of them returned on Monday. 2etebra, v the other at Pope Chateau. from Routes - Rothwn or lakline of road, the one at	

Army Form C. 2118

WAR DIARY or INTELLIGENCE SUMMARY

(Erase heading not required.)

June II

Place	Date	Hour	Summary of Events and Information	Remarks and references to Appendices
26 Av	10/6		O.C. R.E. came over to estimate material for hut & shelved to be built for new dumps, & material indented for. Keys begun to hut. 50 negro prisoners & each & class about 130 strong taken to work. Covered with tarpaulin. Intended to take repairs. Covered with tarpaulin. Work commenced.	
	11/6		600 - 1000 roads. Work commenced. Drainage.	
	12/6		Ditto. C.R.E. inspected unit & dumps.	
	13/6		Pkt Len. Coves at R.Q.M.S. the inspector dumps at same.	
			C.R.A. inspected dumps & shelters. Red running of expected and	
	14/6		Work continued. The Royalist Kr Green moved up to 6.1.8.2 to help them in our war scare.	
	15/6		Recharge. Work continued.	
	16/6		Ditto. Adjutant returns	

A.D.S.S. C.M.Beasly Lt Col

WAR DIARY
or
INTELLIGENCE SUMMARY

Army Form C. 2118

(Erase heading not required.)

Place	Date	Hour	Summary of Events and Information	Remarks and references to Appendices
Lebbeu	17/6		Referred our wife Exploded by an coin in the afternoon. Attacks at Silene & Telouch. S.E. Pepper...	
	18/6		3. S.A.Q. causal replying numbers of enemy artill. At 10 outward retaken a body of 33 and Bat. Sand out Sensorial & 33.20. at 10.30 A.M. H.Q. Leavy Telenor F1... to our line... field 4 letter...	
	19/6		...	

WAR DIARY or INTELLIGENCE SUMMARY

Army Form C. 2118

(Erase heading not required.)

Instructions regarding War Diaries and Intelligence Summaries are contained in F.S. Regs., Part II. and the Staff Manual respectively. Title Pages will be prepared in manuscript.

Place	Date	Hour	Summary of Events and Information	Remarks and references to Appendices
Salonca	21/6		No change.	
	22/6		No change.	
			Route march of A.T. Cypers of C.R.A. & O.C. 30 Div. inspected column on march. Turn out very good. G.O.C. very pleased with turn out & march discipline of Column.	
	23/6		No change. Visited R.A. H.Q.	
	24/6		C.R.A. visited D.A.C. & addressed Indian Conductors. Tactical Exercise for all officers at 6. P.M.	
	25/6		No change.	
	26/6		G.r. Exercise D.A.C. Cease fire 1.10 P.M. Conference at Border W.Q. afterwards reshaw Received. Principal object of scheme was to test the working of ammunition supply under the new organisation of the D.A.C. with the R.A.C. of D.A.C. and generally	

1875 Wt. W593/826 1,000,000 4/15 J.B.C. & A. A.D.S.S./Forms, C. 2118.

Army Form C. 2118

WAR DIARY
or
INTELLIGENCE SUMMARY

(Erase heading not required.)

Instructions regarding War Diaries and Intelligence Summaries are contained in F. S. Regs., Part II. and the Staff Manual respectively. Title Pages will be prepared in manuscript.

Place	Date	Hour	Summary of Events and Information	Remarks and references to Appendices
Jalouue	26/6		I pointed out to L.O.C. that that 53 crawled orderlies out that this was too much for the T.O. to feed. Suggested sheet labour and find orderly for each battery to after the batteries should find the record and the accuracy of ten acquired. Pointed out the necessity of keeping photos in sets to the importance of my personally supervising selections of "A" Echelon wagons. Spoke to OC, as certainly wire too great to allow OC to opt down on a home, of the own care, to be in touch with R. Echelon. Also when Regades moved O Rollins stored the wagon lorry to much the left behind. If my Ammunition has been ordered down to fill the wagons when H.Q. to cartridges for someone during the next report.	
	27/6		No change	
	29/6 7 a.m.	Received orders to come to new area	

1875 Wt. W593/826 1,000,000 4/15 J.B.C. & A. A.D.S.S./Forms/C. 2118.

WAR DIARY
or
INTELLIGENCE SUMMARY
(Erase heading not required.)

Army Form C. 2118

Two

Instructions regarding War Diaries and Intelligence Summaries are contained in F.S. Regs., Part II. and the Staff Manual respectively. Title Pages will be prepared in manuscript.

Place	Date	Hour	Summary of Events and Information	Remarks and references to Appendices
Sollum	28/6		An Officer and Military party known Staff Captain at Sollum about 5 miles N. of total at 5 P.M.	
		12 am	Received intercom we should march on to have killers and Railway crossing at 10.15 P.M. to clear opening at 11 P.M.	
		1.30 P	Noticed over permeable to our own, & was allotted No Envelope village & block of R.T.O.	
			Marched at 9.5 P.M. arrived at head of column at Railway crossing at 10.13 P.M. Advance section held up at Railway crossing by thously Heavier & tail of column therefore delayed, both over 1 hour & whole of column taken. Arrived at our billet	
	29/6		at 3.15 A.M.	
	29/6		No change.	
	29/6		No change.	

C.W. Roche, Lt. Col.

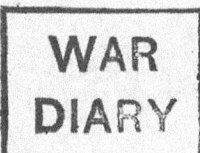

35th DIVISIONAL AMMUNITION COLUMN R.F.A.

1st to 31st JULY 1916.

Vol 6

Confidential

War Diary of
3rd D.A.C.

From 1st July 1916 — 31st July 1916

AH Berkeley

WAR DIARY
or
INTELLIGENCE SUMMARY.

Army Form C. 2118.

General July.

(Erase heading not required.)

Hour, Date, Place	Summary of Events and Information	Remarks and references to Appendices
La Gherloge 1/7/16	Wetage. Visited R.A. Headquarters at Bryas.	
2/7/16	O.C. 2nd Lt. Brooke posted to 163 Bde. Received warning we should probably move during night.	N.B.
3/7/16	Orders received 1.3 a.m. to march to Authieule. Marched at 2 a.m. Arrived at starting point 3.30 a.m. Found great difficulty in breaking horses from water. Reached at 1.30. All arrived. Valued Rocket Aircraft at 4 p.m.	N.B.
4/7/16	Rec'd orders to move at 9.30 a.m. on 5th to Bretel.	N.B.

Army Form C. 2118.

WAR DIARY
or
INTELLIGENCE SUMMARY.

July II

(Erase heading not required.)

Instructions regarding War Diaries and Intelligence Summaries are contained in F. S. Regs., Part II. and the Staff Manual respectively. Title pages will be prepared in manuscript.

Hour, Date, Place	Summary of Events and Information	Remarks and references to Appendices
Authuile - Bouzel 5/7/16	Proceed at 9.20 a.m. Arrived at Bouzel at 11.30 a.m.	
6/7/16	2nd Lt. Barr joined for duty & took up Exchange. C.R.O. called received reports of Raid. Heavy Close action for Lt. Atkinson Capt Philay joined S.O.S. reported to Command 147 Lecken	WB.
7/7/16	C.R.O. wires now being Exchange	WS
8/7/16	Raid orders to move on to at 10.30 a.m.	WS
9/7/16	Proceed to our own at 10.20. Hot period Whole bn ...	WS

(73969) W4141—463. 400,000. 9/14. H.&J.Ltd. Forms/C. 2118/10.

Army Form C. 2118.

WAR DIARY
or
INTELLIGENCE SUMMARY.

(Erase heading not required.)

July III

Instructions regarding War Diaries and Intelligence Summaries are contained in F.S. Regs., Part II. and the Staff Manual respectively. Title pages will be prepared in manuscript.

Hour, Date, Place	Summary of Events and Information	Remarks and references to Appendices
9/7/16. Authie.	at Authie. Received orders to march on Authie. Arrived about 1.30 P.M	AYB.
10/7/16	Recd orders f. P.A.C. Kester of Fortée to go forward. Orders subsequently changed — received fresh orders f. a/a of Sec S. of A.C. to march to Varennes. Reached at 9.30 P.M.	AYB
11/7/16 Varennes.	Arrived Varennes at 1.30 A.M., & left again at 10 A.M. f. Hillencourt arrived about 1.30 P.M. G.R.A. called in the afternoon. In charge Various R.A. Fg	AYB GJ Ruby W.R.A
12/7/16		

(73989) W4141—463. 400,000. 9/14. H.&J.Ltd. Forms/C. 2118/10.

Army Form C. 2118.

WAR DIARY
or
INTELLIGENCE SUMMARY.

(Erase heading not required.)

July IV

Hour, Date, Place	Summary of Events and Information	Remarks and references to Appendices
Millencourt 13/7/16	2nd Lts Gregg & G. Hardy joined & posted to 1, 4 and No 3 Sections respectively. Received sudden orders to leave immediately. Movement at 6.30 P.M. where we should be told our Camp to Moulincourt. On arrival at Moulincourt we were ordered on to Bois de Taille. Reports to Camp Commandant had great difficulty in finding him as it is a very large camp & absolutely no directions or sign posts up. This enabled nicely to done. Consequently we did not get into Camp at about 10 P.M. Picked ammunition dump which we were to	A.H. Parker Lt Col

Army Form C. 2118.

WAR DIARY
or
INTELLIGENCE SUMMARY.

(Erase heading not required.)

July

Hour, Date, Place	Summary of Events and Information	Remarks and references to Appendices
Bois de Taillees R.10 cent. Sheet 62D	Take over fm 9th Div. near Bray	
14/7/16	Reported afternoon to G.O.C. H.Q.	OWB
15/7/16	Established H.Q. forward dump at Carnoy, but reported themselves "short"	OWB
16th	No change. 2 2nd Lieutenants joined. H.Q. arrived.	OWB
	Remainder of F.O.O. arrived	OWB
17/7/16	No change	OWB
	2 2nd Lieuts posted to No 3 Co. F.O.O.	OWB
18/7/16	No change	OWB
19/7/16	No change	OWB
20/7/16	Moved to new Dump at Bray — Albert road	OWB

WAR DIARY
or
INTELLIGENCE SUMMARY.
(Erase heading not required.)

Army Form C. 2118.

July ZZ

Hour, Date, Place	Summary of Events and Information	Remarks and references to Appendices
K.26.a.2.1. 20/7/16 21/7/16	at K.26.a.2.1. Kept up own from 20 in. At 2 below Optr Dro Keaun Issued B.6115.a. S117 ax 2424 Rt.	AW
	198 Wayn Teams at	AWB.
22/7/16	Very heavy issue of ammunition 21527 a 6717 at 6384 Rt 190 Teen a total of 30826 teams. 325 Wagon Teams out.	AW
23/7/16	Ammunition Reckoning 22 842 rounds 223 Wagn Teams out.	AW
24/7/16	2nd Lt Robt C.M. Rahn ill retained to Field Ambulance Ammunition Supplied 16862 rounds 182 Teams	AW M.M. Ruby 7/Col

WAR DIARY or INTELLIGENCE SUMMARY.

Army Form C. 2118.

July

Hour, Date, Place	Summary of Events and Information	Remarks and references to Appendices
F.26.d.21 Map Ref. 62.D. 25/7/16 2nd Army	Ammunition supplied 13230 rounds 232 Wagon Teams out. Received orders to send up 6 x 2 wh G.S. Carts R. Hardy to report T/ C. Turner to 157 Bde. to replace casualties	AHB
26/7/16	Ammunition supplied 16074 rounds 6 Wagon Teams out 176 2 /Lt. G.S. Katt returned to T.O. Lce/Cpl. S3 Jeames to replace casualties	AHB AHB
27/7/16	Issued 21,022 rounds C.R.A. visited dump. Teams out 232	AHB
28/7/16	Issued 17408 rounds Teams out 139 Supplied total of 40 Officers remounts a week	AHB AHB AHB

WAR DIARY or **INTELLIGENCE SUMMARY.**

Army Form C. 2118.

July 1916

(Erase heading not required.)

Instructions regarding War Diaries and Intelligence Summaries are contained in F.S. Regs., Part II. and the Staff Manual respectively. Title pages will be prepared in manuscript.

Hour, Date, Place	Summary of Events and Information	Remarks and references to Appendices
F.26.a.2.1 Ref. 62.D.		
28/7/16	Visited R.A.O.D. near Billon Farm. Capt. Crooks all returned to Brick Works	ONB
	to No 3 Res. S.A.D.	ONB
29/7/16	Issued 17330 rounds 160 Cloja Teamwork	ONB
30/7/16	Supplied 22192 rounds 201 Teams out Sent 2 wagons from child pa.	ONB
31/7/16	Supplied 15788 rounds 154 Teams out	ONB

35th Divisional Artillery

35th DIVISIONAL AMMUNITION COLUMN. R.F.A.

AUGUST 1 9 1 6

Army Form C. 2118.

Vol 7

WAR DIARY
or
INTELLIGENCE SUMMARY.
(Erase heading not required.)

Confidential

War Diary
of
35. B.F.A.C.

From Aug. 1. 1916 to Aug 31. 1916.
(Volume 7)

A. Park Lt. Col.
Comdg 35 B.F.A.C.

WAR DIARY or INTELLIGENCE SUMMARY

Army Form C. 2118.

August 1916

Hour, Date, Place	Summary of Events and Information	Remarks and references to Appendices
Map Reference 62D FILLIEFORME TREE F.26.A.2.1. Aug. 1. 1916.	The following casualties were notified from War Diary, July 26th: 1 Driver killed. July 29. 1 Driver killed, 1 Primary 2 Wounded. "B" Echelon ordered to move to W. of MEAULTE	
Aug. 2.	"B" Echelon ordered A.332.A. 1960.A.X. 1000 B.X. Sheet. moved 3056.A. 12.16.A.X. 1000 B.X. Transferred to 30 Jan 30 58.A. near Corps Echelon. Ordered to move H.Q. to 55 J.Q.P. namely Handed our Dump to 46 B. 2614 B.X. Sheet 4336.A. 2324.A.X. 46 B. R.A.G. fevers etc. Lechons No 2 and 3 attached for duty to "B's. A.D." No 1 and 4 to 2nd D.A.C. Three H.Q. k. E.?? A. 5.2 Right k. 63 D. DERNANCOURT Following officers proceed 2nd LT G.P. DOUGLAS Sgt B	

WAR DIARY
or
INTELLIGENCE SUMMARY.

Army Form C. 2118.

August 1916

(Erase heading not required.)

Hour, Date, Place	Summary of Events and Information	Remarks and references to Appendices
S. of DERNANCOURT E 27 a 5.2 Map Ref. 62D Aug. 2 Cont.	2ⁿᵈ Lt: F. R FORSTER and 2ⁿᵈ Lt N.H. HANNA CAPT. A.M. CAVE C.F. joined from 1st Rde.	A.H. Ray. OC 4B.
Aug 3.	No change	
Aug 4.	No change 2ⁿᵈ Lt G. P DOUGLAS posted to 157 Bde 2ⁿᵈ Lt F. R FORSTER posted to 158 Bde 2ⁿᵈ Lt N.H. HANNA posted to 159 Bde 2ⁿᵈ Lt L.A. DENISON posted to Div. Am Base.	A.H.B.
Aug. 5	No change 2ⁿᵈ Lt A. P. JOHNSTONE proceeded to England to report to War Office ENGLAND	A.H.B.

Lt. COL. F.F.A. COM.D.G. 52ⁿᵈ D.A.C.

WAR DIARY
or
INTELLIGENCE SUMMARY.

Army Form C. 2118.

August 1916

Hour, Date, Place	Summary of Events and Information	Remarks and references to Appendices
S. of DERNANCOURT		
27 a.5.2.D	2nd Lt. L.A. DENISON posted to	
Ref Ref 62 D	157 Bde. R.F.A.	AHB.
Aug 5th Cal.	No change	AHB.
Aug 6th	No change	
Aug 7th	No change	
	Lt. T. MACLAGAN attached to 157 Bde	AHB.
	2nd Lt. W.A. GREGG " " 159 "	AHB.
	2nd Lt. D.W.H. JOHNSON " " 163 "	AHB.
	2nd Lt. G.D.G. SCOTT " " 158 "	AHB.
	2nd Lt. F.R. SMITH " " 159 "	
Aug 8	No change	
Aug 9	No change. Very hot indeed.	
Aug 10.	Raining. No change.	

WAR DIARY or INTELLIGENCE SUMMARY

Army Form C. 2118.

August 1916

(Erase heading not required.)

Hour, Date, Place	Summary of Events and Information	Remarks and references to Appendices
S. of DERNANCOURT E.27.a.5.2. Sheet 62.D. *Night of Aug. 11*	No change.	
Aug. 12	No change. 2nd Lt. T. C. TURNER reported for attachment to 157 Bde. No 2 Sec. returned from being attached to the 157.	A43. A43.
Aug. 13	5/9 A.C. Staff decided to elect a Sir Officers' Mess Committee of present members, + Col. BERLY ? was appointed Pres. and 2 officers to be appointed from each Section to serve on the Committee.	A43.
Aug. 14	Repairs to D.A.C. No change. Lt. B. W. INGRAM posted to No 9 Sec.	

D.A. M?Kerlie
Lt. Col. R.F.A.
Comdg. 35th D.A.C.

WAR DIARY
or
INTELLIGENCE SUMMARY

(Erase heading not required.)

Army Form C. 2118.

August 1916.

Hour, Date, Place	Summary of Events and Information	Remarks and references to Appendices
S.O.F. DERNANCOURT E27 a.5.2.D Lat.Ref. 62D Aug 14 Contd.	2/Lt. T.H. CAMERON posted to D.A.C. Appeared from 149 Bde. Artillery with personnel Will-recuck further Batteries with personnel posted up to a.p. the following officers belong to T.M. batteries joined later on the strength, but supernumerary to establishment. 2/Lt. A.B. WHALEY } X. T.M. Bty 2/Lt. H.M. HEADLEY } Lt. P.R. LURCOTT } Y. T.M. Bty 2/Lt. T.R. GUYER } 2/Lt. A.C. DAVIDSON } Z. T.M. Bty 2/Lt. E.A. LOWE } No 3 Coy. Returned from being attached to St. D.A.C. G.O.C. 30th Div. called & addressed men	A.N.B. O.H. Newbury Lt Col RFA G.O.C. 30 Div Arty

Aug 15.

WAR DIARY
INTELLIGENCE SUMMARY

Army Form C. 2118.

August 1916

Hour, Date, Place	Summary of Events and Information	Remarks and references to Appendices
1st Bn DERNANCOURT E.27.a.d.2 Ref Ref 62D Aug 15 contd	2/Lt T.A.C. DAVIDSON went to hospital for rec. sickness from being attached to 2.F.A. as 12th Reint.	A.W.B.
Aug 16.	For rec attached duty to 2nd F.A.	
Aug 17.	No. 2 " 2.F.A. Lancer 1024 A Coy A.X. 528 B+ Lt. E.T. CORRAN taken to Co. Adjutant hospital rewounds to the R.C. Clats Lances 1240. T. P. X to 2nd 3rd & 5th A.L.G.H.R.	A.W.B. A.W.B.
Aug 18.	Lancer 374 P.X to g. T.N.9. Lt. B.W. INGRAM fm 159 Rec reported to D.A.O.H armed column. 2/Lt. E.D.G. SCOTT Rated to 1st Bn 2/Lt LEWIS etta. Dir. Bomb. Here	

A.W. ...... R.F.A.
Comdg 1st Bn

WAR DIARY
or
INTELLIGENCE SUMMARY.
(Erase heading not required.)

August 1916 Army Form C. 2118.

VII

Hour, Date, Place	Summary of Events and Information	Remarks and references to Appendices
St ADERNANCOURT 57.a.d.2 Ref 62D Aug 19	2/Lt E.T. CORRAN wounded by Plane	
	No ammunition issued.	
Aug 20.	No change.	A.V.B. Col.
	No change.	
Aug 21.	No change. Lt INGRAM attd to 5" Ind Rest Res.	
	No change. Issued 1056 Q. 352 QK 250 RX Orders received that T.M. Batteries are to be reorganised looking: X to B2 Y. to B2 2 to B3 2/Lt F.R. SMITH posted to 109 R.L. 2/Lt F.R. SMITH posted to 109 R.L.	A.V.B.
Aug 22	No change CRO called. 2/Lt CAMERON ex L^t hospital. Received orders to hand over T.M. Batteries. Issued 520Q. 1768x 276 mills grenades	A.V.B.

WAR DIARY or INTELLIGENCE SUMMARY

Army Form C. 2118.

(Erase heading not required.)

Army August 1916   VIII

Hour, Date, Place	Summary of Events and Information	Remarks and references to Appendices
S. of DERNANCOURT E 27 a 5.2 Map Ref 1/62D Aug. 23.	No change. 7 M Patterson went into action Spare O2 Bk 2/Lt Lee returned from his attachment to 2/70 Bde	AWB
Aug. 24	No change Reported Act H.Q. role inspected Rout ?. Hone at the Camp C. CITADEL	AWB
Aug. 25.	No change Spencer 11.00 A 30 4 A X. 107 BX No change Spares inspection 2/Lt Lee returned from being attached to 3 Bde	
Aug. 26	7 M Batteries returned. 2/Lt TOMLINSON rejoined Column / 152 Bde 2.30 2/Lt G.M. HOOLFON Hand J.M.S. WRIGHT. joined from Base Attached to B. Battery	

WAR DIARY
or
INTELLIGENCE SUMMARY

Army Form C. 2118.

August 1916   IX

Hour, Date, Place	Summary of Events and Information	Remarks and references to Appendices
C. of DERMANCOURT		
F.27 a.5.2		
Sht Ref 62D		
Aug. 27	No change.	
Aug 28	Raining hard. Hensdictown. No change.	OK/S
	Several porters left for unknown destination.	OK/S
Aug 29	Rainy. Very bad roads, kept wind. Orders read direct from Corps for very heavy fatigues. 15 Wagons to GROVETOWN for today's ammunition. 15 to Colincamps supply certes, canvas etc. 20 to go to CARNOY to Heavies. These latter went up and waited till 9 P.M. but did nothing received. Issued 264 Rx.	OK/S
Aug. 30	Received orders to fill up. Collected teams. All fan ammunition required by Column.	

C.J. Reid
LT. COL. R.F.A.
COMDG. 35th D.A.C.

WAR DIARY
or
INTELLIGENCE SUMMARY.

Army Form C. 2118.

August 1916

(Erase heading not required.)

Hour, Date, Place	Summary of Events and Information	Remarks and references to Appendices
5.27 a.s.2 Sh of Ref 62D Aug 31	No change. Recd orders we should move Sept 3rd. Filled up with powder (4,400) Heavy fatigues again. Had 3 wagons destroyed by shell fire yesterday in Carnoy Valley. CARNOY VALLEY	[signature] Col 35th S.B.

Vol 8

Army Form C. 2118.

WAR DIARY
~~INTELLIGENCE SUMMARY.~~
(Erase heading not required.)

Instructions regarding War Diaries and Intelligence Summaries are contained in F. S. Regs., Part II. and the Staff Manual respectively. Title pages will be prepared in manuscript.

Hour, Date, Place	Summary of Events and Information	Remarks and references to Appendices
	Confidential War Diary 35 B.A.C. From Sept 1. 1916 — Sept 30. 1916 (Volume 8)	

Army Form C. 2118.

WAR DIARY
or
INTELLIGENCE SUMMARY

(Erase heading not required.)

September 1916

Instructions regarding War Diaries and Intelligence Summaries are contained in F.S. Regs., Part II. and the Staff Manual respectively. Title pages will be prepared in manuscript.

Hour, Date, Place	Summary of Events and Information	Remarks and references to Appendices
S.S. DERNANCOURT Map Ref. 62D E.27.a.5.2.	In charge. Made Art H.Q. Was informed enemy preparing to attack or one tell off. Rather doubtful.	
Sept 1.	Lt. MACLAGAN attached 157 Bde. In charge. Received orders to move tonight. Subsequently this order was cancelled.	OMB
Sept 2.	Ordered to move Sept 3. Gone in arrears, heavy rain afterwards.	OMB
Sept 3.	Marched at 9.10 A.M. Arrived at Starting point MORLANCOURT at 9.50. Reached billets for night. Namely DAOURS	
DAOURS.	at 3 P.M. Billets good, town never had been exposed to shell fire. Received orders to check fitting afternoon	O M Berly Lt. Col. R.F.A. Commdg. 35th D.A.O.

(73939) W4141—463. 400,000. 9/14. H.&J.Ltd. Forms/C. 2118/10.

WAR DIARY or INTELLIGENCE SUMMARY

Army Form C. 2118.

September 1916

(Erase heading not required.)

Instructions regarding War Diaries and Intelligence Summaries are contained in F.S. Regs., Part II. and the Staff Manual respectively. Title pages will be prepared in manuscript.

Hour, Date, Place	Summary of Events and Information	Remarks and references to Appendices
DAOURS – RAINNEVILLE Sept 4th	Marched at 2 P.M. to RAINNEVILLE near VILLERS BOCAGE arriving at about 5.30 P.M. Horse lines food, also officers. Received orders to march next morning to BOISBERGUES.	
Sept 5 RAINNEVILLE – BOISBERGUES	Dull but fine much laer. Marched at 10 a.m. to BOISBERGUES. Arrived about 6 P.M. Delayed along the line at Bt & bridge, window in Ercely Wy Bge & bricks on in Ercely. Watered & fed at 1 P.M. at Rent opp. Watered & fed at [illegible] Paper shew CAMAPLES. 1 mile Paper shew Pellets had of late only windrople. Horse lines had not yet been vacated by 17th. Recd. ready to march tomorrow to REMAISN. Brielle to Beauval – MEZEROLLES	[signature] Lt Col RFA Comdg. 35th DAC

WAR DIARY September 1916 Army Form C. 2118.

or

INTELLIGENCE SUMMARY.

(Erase heading not required.)

Hour, Date, Place	Summary of Events and Information	Remarks and references to Appendices
Sept 6th BOISBERGUES - REMAISNIL	Marched to REMAISNIL at 11 A.M. A Echelon billeted there. B at MEZEROLLES. Arriving at about 1 P.M. Lines shelter good. C.R.A. called in afternoon. Weather fine.	
Sept 7 REMAISNIL - LUCHEUX	Marched at 3.30 P.M. to LUCHEUX arriving about 6 P.M. Fine day. C.R.Q. walked Column march parket BOUQUEMAISON. Received orders to march next day to MONTENESCOURT, & to report TOWN MAJOR there. Appointed 2/Lt. T.E.G. HEAVEY.	
Sept 8th LUCHEUX - MONTENESCOURT	Fine. Marched at 8.30 a.m. to MONTENESCOURT. Personally driven over C.R.A.'s car. Column marched under orders of Capt. WILKINSON	

Army Form C. 2118.

WAR DIARY
or
INTELLIGENCE SUMMARY.
(Erase heading not required.)

September 1916. IV

Instructions regarding War Diaries and Intelligence Summaries are contained in F.S. Regs., Part II. and the Staff Manual respectively. Title pages will be prepared in manuscript.

Hour, Date, Place	Summary of Events and Information	Remarks and references to Appendices
Sept 8. 1916. LUCHEUX - MONTENES- COURT. Contd.	Personally arrived at MONTENESCOURT at 11.30 A.M. & took over Arms for Lt Col. AM= DERSON. Awaiting to 382 A.X. the few hours. Handed over to his S.A.R. Lt. Sar at LUCHEUX. 2500 A. 4 AX 1362 BX Column arrived about 4 P.M. Men & horses are very fit.	
MONTENESCOURT Sept 9.	Fine. No change.	AWB
Sept 10.	Fine. No change. Issued 244 A. 290 AX 383 BX	AWB
Sept 11.	Fine. No change. S.O.C. 35th Div called. Issued 624 BX 26 B.P.F.	AWB
Sept 12	No change. Lt Col. BERRY went on leave. CAPT WILKINSON takes over Command	AWB

A W Butler
LT. COL. R.F.A.
COMDG. 35th D.A.C.

WAR DIARY or INTELLIGENCE SUMMARY.

Army Form C. 2118.

September 1916.

Hour, Date, Place	Summary of Events and Information	Remarks and references to Appendices
MONTENESCOURT Sept 12 contd.	LIEUT KILPATRICK sent to Albany T.M. School. 2nd Lt CAMERON struck off strength. Issued 260 RA 20 B.P.F.	OMB.
Sept 13	Heavy rain. Capt CROXALL went on leave Capt. CROXALL Issued 1380-A 578 AX 460 B 340-BX 22 B.P.F.	OMB
Sept 14	Rec'd orders to move to WANQUETIN on 15th In Charge Issued 9317 A 9914 X 47 BX 30 B.P.F.	OMB
Sept 15	Move to WANQUETIN at 1 P.M. as ordered.	
WANQUETIN	Could not get into lines as batteries had not all moved out. Issued 1240 722 AX 496 BX.	OM Rey

LT. COL. CONDG. 35th R.F.A.

WAR DIARY
or
INTELLIGENCE SUMMARY.

(Erase heading not required.)

Army Form C. 2118.

September 1916

Hour, Date, Place	Summary of Events and Information	Remarks and references to Appendices
WANQUETIN Sept 16.	Moved section that could not get into their proper lines yesterday into their proper lines. Issued 600 a. 1284 ax. 156 Rx	OWB
Sept 17	Issued 600 a. 264 ax.	OWB
Sept 18.	No change. Started heavy fatigues loading coal &c. for civilians. Raining hard. B/Lr B/Lr O'DONNELL & Co. HASTED worked the lines. Issued 177 Rx.	OWB
Sept 19	No change. Issued 363 a.	OWB
Sept 20	Capt. MILNE went on leave. No change.	OWB

Akerly
LT. COL. R.F.A.
COMDG. 35th D.A.C.

WAR DIARY
or
INTELLIGENCE SUMMARY.

(Erase heading not required.)

Army Form C. 2118.

September 1916.

Hour, Date, Place	Summary of Events and Information	Remarks and references to Appendices
WANQUETIN		
Sept 21	LIEUT. CURRAN reported from ENGLAND. Joined 96 Bty.	AHB
Sept 22	LT. COL. BERLY reported having had to stay 1 day in BOULOGNE. D.D.V.S. inspected all horses & mules. Joined 252 Bty.	
Sept 23	No change	AHB
Sept 24	CAPT. SMITH & 2nd LT. TURNER went on leave.	AHB
Sept 25	O.R.A. called.	AHB
Sept 26	Joined 585 Q. 791 OX.	AHB
Sept 27	No change	AHB

AWBerly
LT. COL. R.F.A.
COMDG. 35th D.A.C.

WAR DIARY
or
INTELLIGENCE SUMMARY.
(Erase heading not required.)

Army Form C. 2118.

September 1916

VII

Hour, Date, Place	Summary of Events and Information	Remarks and references to Appendices
WANQUETIN		
Sept 28	Capt WILKINSON & 2nd Lt HEADLEY and 2nd Lt MOORE went on leave.	
Sept 29	Issued 96 RX.	
Sept 30	Issued 220 QX, 100 RX. Moved Headquarters from CHATEAU to MAYORS HOUSE which was kept close to Section. Dugouts for Telephone Stations have progressed very satisfactorily during the month.	

[signature]
LT. COL. R.F.A.
COMDG. 35th D.A.C.

Army Form C. 2118.

Vol 4

WAR DIARY
or
INTELLIGENCE SUMMARY

(*Erase heading not required.*)

Confidential

War Diary
35 B.A.C.
Oct 1. 1916 — Oct 31. 1916
From Oct 1. 1916 — Oct 31 1916
(Volume 7)

A.W. Parker Lt. Col. R.F.A.
Comdg 35 B.A.C.

WAR DIARY or INTELLIGENCE SUMMARY

Army Form C. 2118.

(Erase heading not required.)

Place	Date	Hour	Summary of Events and Information	Remarks and references to Appendices
MANQUETIN	Oct 1		No change. Joined 324 A 1040 Ax	
	" 2		" Issued 96 Bx	
	" 3		" 2/Lt PRICE Went on leave	
	" 4		Capt SMITH and 2/Lt TURNER returned from Leave. Issued 120 Bx	
	" 5		Gen Staff STAVELEY called to h.qrs. Competition for test turnout and best Rolled Rolls.	
	" 6		No change. 2/Lt CHAMBERS joined from BASE	
	" 7		2/Lt BARNETT and Lt INGLIS went on leave. Issued 152 Ax 48 Bx	

Army Form C. 2118.

WAR DIARY
or
INTELLIGENCE SUMMARY

(Erase heading not required.)

October 1916

Place	Date	Hour	Summary of Events and Information	Remarks and references to Appendices
WANQUETIN	8		No Change	OMR
	9		Capt WILKINSON returned from leave. Murphey dump started at L.q.d.s.s. War DUISANS Issued 8008x	OMR
	10		Gen LANDON and Brig. Gen. STAVELEY inspected all cook houses and latrines. Col HASTED and D.A.D.O.S. inspected men's clothing. Supplied horse for recce CORPS EQUITATION SCHOOL at HAUTEVILLE. 2/Lt MOORE struck off strength. Issued 150 4x 1440 Br	OMR
	11		No Change	OMR
	12		Lt Col BERLY evacuated to hospital. Capt WILKINSON	OMR

2449 Wt. W14957/M90 750,000 1/16 J.B.C. & A. Form/C.2118/12.

Army Form C. 2118.

WAR DIARY
or
INTELLIGENCE SUMMARY

(Erase heading not required.)

October 1916

Place	Date	Hour	Summary of Events and Information	Remarks and references to Appendices
WANQUETIN	12		Taken over Command. "Lt LEWIS went on leave. Issued 524Hx 240 Bx	
	13		No Change. Issued 100 BPF	
	14		" "Lt PRICE returned from leave. Issued 224A	
	15		Issued A49 Hx 240 Bx	
	16		Capt E.R. TONGUE - CROXALL absented themselves town Major of ARRAS. Issued 224Hx 120 Bx	
	17		No Change. Issued 234Hx 120 Bx	
	18		"Lt BARNETT returns from leave. Received horse Reserve	

WAR DIARY
or
INTELLIGENCE SUMMARY

(Erase heading not required.)

Army Form C. 2118.

October 1916.

Place	Date	Hour	Summary of Events and Information	Remarks and references to Appendices
WANQUETIN	18 (Cont)		That Lt Col BERLY has proceeded to ENGLAND. Issued 673 AX	M/y
	19		Lt CURRAN resigns as Adjutant and ceased to act as. Issued 124 BX	M/y
			Lt INGLIS returned from leave.	
	20		No change. Issued 120 BX	M/y
	21		No change	M/y
	22		Lt HEANEY went on leave. Issued 209 AX, 180 BX	M/y
	23		A.D.V.S. inspected all horses and lines.	M/y
	24		Lt LEWIS returned from leave. Issued 225 A, 700 AX	M/y
	25		No change. Issued 120 BX	M/y

WAR DIARY or INTELLIGENCE SUMMARY

Army Form C. 2118.

October 1916

Place	Date	Hour	Summary of Events and Information	Remarks and references to Appendices
WANQUETIN	26		2/Lt BARNETT appointed Adjutant with effect from 19.10.16	MB
	27		2/Lt JOHNSON went on leave. Issued 262 AX 836 HX	MB
	28		No change. Issued 360 A 1184 HX 4508 HX	MB
	29		No change. Issued 448 A 228 AX 440 BX 2/Lt FOSTER joined from B1 HSE	MB
	30		2/Lt Col BERLY returned from ENGLAND. Issued 2054 A 803 AX 534 BPF 350 BX	WB
	31		No change. Issued 228 A 76 AX	WB

Army Form C. 2118.

WAR DIARY
or
INTELLIGENCE SUMMARY
(Erase heading not required.)

Vol 10

Confidential

War Diary
35 D.A.C.
From Nov 1st 1916 — Nov 30th 1916
(Volume 10)

Appendix (N°40)
Cmdt 35 D.A.C.

WAR DIARY or INTELLIGENCE SUMMARY

Army Form C. 2118.

November 1916

Place	Date	Hour	Summary of Events and Information	Remarks and references to Appendices
	Nov		HEANEY	
NANQUETIN	1		No Change. 2Lt Heaney returned from leave. Rained	AWB
K32	2		No Change. Dull day	AWB
Sheet 51CNE	3		" Issued 304 H 764 X Rained hard	AWB
	4		" 458 H 226 AX 300 BX	AWB
	5		No Change	AWB
	6		2Lt JOHNSON returned from leave. Issued 220 AY 9682	AWB
	7		2Lt TURNER returned to duty from hospital. Rained much	AWB
	8		No Change. Issued 1404 X 100 BX Capt M°KNATT returned to duty from leave acting Town Major ARRAS	AWB

Army Form C. 2118.

WAR DIARY
or
INTELLIGENCE SUMMARY

(Erase heading not required.)

November 1916

Instructions regarding War Diaries and Intelligence Summaries are contained in F. S. Regs., Part II. and the Staff Manual respectively. Title Pages will be prepared in manuscript.

Place	Date	Hour	Summary of Events and Information	Remarks and references to Appendices
WANQUETIN K.32.d Sh:57SIGNE	8 (continued)		2/Lt A R JOHNSTON reported B/159 from Engineers duty with DAC.	OWB
	9		No Change. Fine day	OWB
	10		" Issued 5740 BX	OWB
	11		Capt J BAIRD C.F. joined.	OWB
	12		No change. Issued 120 BX	OWB
	13		"	OWB
	14		2/Lt L W BARNETT Promoted Lt and appointed Adjutant from 19.10.16. 2/Lt RICHARDSON rejoined B/58 from Temporary duty Offr.	OWB
	15		No Change.	OWB

Army Form C. 2118.

WAR DIARY
or
INTELLIGENCE SUMMARY

(Erase heading not required.)

November 1916

Place	Date	Hour	Summary of Events and Information	Remarks and references to Appendices
WIANQUETIN	Nov 16		No Change. Issued 38 PH 190 Ax	(A) 443
K32	17		No change. Fine day. Competition for best turn out in column	
Blairsierre			Major Gen. LANDON C.B. aud Brig Gen. STANLEY C.B. judged gues	
	18		No Change. 2/Lt C.A. LEWIS promoted Lt from 2.9.16	(A) P
	19		No Change	(A) P
	20		Issued 60 PAK	(A) P
	21		2/Lt PRICE to Hospital	(A) P
	22		No change. Issued 970 Ax 192 BX	(A) P
	23		ADVS inspected horses of 1-2. 73 Letters	(A) P

WAR DIARY or INTELLIGENCE SUMMARY

Army Form C. 2118.

November 1916

Place	Date	Hour	Summary of Events and Information	Remarks and references to Appendices
WANDOETTE	24		No Change. 2Lt WOOLNOUGH went on leave	
K32 Sh.51CNE	25		" Lt. C.A. LEWIS to hospital. 152 AX 270 BX lanchy	OWB
	26		" Issued 76A 869AX 138 BX	OWB
	27		" 2Lt G.D. SCOTT posted from 7B5 to 157 Bde	OWB
			Issued 303 AX 306 BX	OWB
	28		" No Change. Issued 152 A 5964 X	OWB
	29		"	OWB
	30		" Issued 228 A 96 BX. 2Lt HEADLEY X/B5-6	
			157 Bde. 2Lt E.M. LECKIE X/B5 to 157 157 Bde to X/B5 TNB	

Lt. Col. Comdg. R.F.A.

Army Form C. 2118.

WAR DIARY
or
INTELLIGENCE SUMMARY.
(Erase heading not required.)

Instructions regarding War Diaries and Intelligence Summaries are contained in F.S. Regs., Part II. and the Staff Manual respectively. Title pages will be prepared in manuscript.

Hour, Date, Place	Summary of Events and Information	Remarks and references to Appendices

Confidential

War Diary

35 D.A.C.

From Dec 1st 1916 - Dec 31st 1916

(Volume II)

Army Form C. 2118.

WAR DIARY
or
INTELLIGENCE SUMMARY.
(Erase heading not required.)

December 1916

Hour, Date, Place	Summary of Events and Information	Remarks and references to Appendices
WANQUETIN K.32.b.5of5ignE 1.12.16	No change. Issued 76 A	OWB
2. " "	2Lt Robertson RICHARDSON posted from 158 Bde	OWB
" "	2Lt F.R. FOSTER posted to 158 Bde. Issued 144 Bx	OWB
3. " "	No change	OWB
4. " "	Issued 672 A + 52 Bx	OWB
5. " "	Issued 698 A + 889 13x	OWB
6. " "	Issued 1058 A 1068 A + 920 Bx	OWB
7. " "	Issued 1122 A + 202 13x. 2Lt PRICE proceeded to ETAPLES for dental treatment	OWB
8. " "	Issued Nil. 2Lt WOOLNOUGH returned from leave	OWB
9. " "	2Lt J.M.S. WRIGHT went on leave. Issued 100 A 162 A + 40 B PF 300 Bx	OWB

O.W. Burle Lt Col

Army Form C. 2118.

WAR DIARY
INTELLIGENCE SUMMARY.
(Erase heading not required.)

December 1916

Instructions regarding War Diaries and Intelligence Summaries are contained in F. S. Regs., Part II. and the Staff Manual respectively. Title pages will be prepared in manuscript.

Hour, Date, Place	Summary of Events and Information	Remarks and references to Appendices
WANQUETIN K.32.5 NE 10.12.16	No change	
11.12.16	Issued 704 A× 10 B×	
12 " "	Issued 228 13 Pl N	
13 " "	Issued 422 A 1306 A× 288 R×	
14 " "	Issued 524 R× 122 N 32 N×	
15 " "	Issued 352 A 892 A× 158 R× 458 N 76 N×	
16 " "	Issued 227 A× 205 BPF 511 R×	
17 " "	Lt Col BERLY Went on leave Issued 5 BPF 1252× Capt WILKINSON assumed Command	
18 " "	No change	
19 " "	Issued 224 H 672 A× 360 B× 2/Lt JMS WRIGHT returned from leave	
20 " "	Issued 348 N 4 N×	

Army Form C. 2118.

WAR DIARY
INTELLIGENCE SUMMARY.
(Erase heading not required.)

December 1916

Hour, Date, Place		Summary of Events and Information	Remarks and references to Appendices
WANQUETIN K32.51 c N E	21.12.16	Issued 2044 A 1988 A 768 Bx. 2/Lt PRICE rejoined from hospital	AKB
	22 " "	" 456 A 4442 Ax 3174 Bx	AKB
	23 " "	" 248 A 2080 Ax 460 N 128 Nx	AKB
	24 " "	No change	AKB
	25 " "	Issued 168 N 48 Nx 2/Lt CLARK joined from 12th Div. on first Brunswick. 2/Lt WOOLNOUGH posted to 159 Bde.	AKB
	26 " "	Issued 376 Ax 530 Bx. 2/Lt RICHARDSON went on leave. 2/Lt CLARK went to hospital. Column moved from WANQUETIN to REBREUVIETTE	AKB
REBREUVIETTE M6 central Sheet 51C	27 " "	Lt Col BERRY returned from leave	AKB
	28 " "	No change	AKB

WAR DIARY

INTELLIGENCE SUMMARY.

(Erase heading not required.)

Army Form C. 2118.

December 1916

Hour, Date, Place	Summary of Events and Information	Remarks and references to Appendices
REBREUVIETTE M.6 Central Sheet 51C. { 29.12.16 30 " " 31 " "	No change " "	

Army Form C. 2118.

WAR DIARY
or
INTELLIGENCE SUMMARY.
(Erase heading not required.)

Vol 12

Confidential

War Diary

3rd D.Ba.C

From January 1st - January 31st 1917

(Volume 12)

WAR DIARY

INTELLIGENCE SUMMARY
(Erase heading not required.)

Army Form C. 2118

January 1917

Place	Date	Hour	Summary of Events and Information	Remarks and references to Appendices
REBREUVIETTE M.6 Central Sheet 51C	Jan 1		No Change	MB
	2		" "	MB
	3		No 2 Sec reconstructed	MB
	4		No Change	MB
	5		2.Lt CLARK struck off strength on being evacuated sick to ENGLAND	MB
	6		2.Lt RICHARDSON returned from leave	MB
	7		No 1 Sec and No 3 Sec moved to BOURET M 36 a 8 (51C)	MB
	8		No Change	MB
BOURET M.3.b.9.8 51C	9		Hd qrs & No 2 Sec moved to BOURET. No 3 Sec moved to MONTENESCOURT	MB

WAR DIARY
or
INTELLIGENCE SUMMARY.

Army Form C. 2118.

January 1917

II

Hour, Date, Place	Summary of Events and Information	Remarks and references to Appendices
BOURET M.3.b.9.8. 51C January 9	35th D.A.C. details proceeded to 48 A.F.A. B.A.C. and 52 A.F.A. B.A.C. 2/Lt WRIGHT posted to 157 Bde	MO
10	Capt CROXALL proceeded on leave. Remainder of details went to 64 A.F.A B.A.C.	MO
11	A.O.rS on speed tores of K.O 1 & 2 Batteries	MO
12	Provisional Gas Officer inspected all Box Helmets. Reorganisation of D.A.C. completed	MO
13	No change	MO
14	No change	MO
WANQUETIN K.32.c 51CNE 15	HQ moved to WANQUETIN and No 1 to MONTENESCOURT and took over Ammunition Supply. Capt WILKINSON took over Command vice Lt Col BENNY on PARIS leave. Issued 608A×	

Army Form C. 2118.

WAR DIARY
INTELLIGENCE SUMMARY
(Erase heading not required.)

January 1917

Hour, Date, Place	Summary of Events and Information	Remarks and references to Appendices
WANQUETIN K32C SIGNE 16	2/Lt F.G. LEAMAN 2/Lt MACGREGOR 2/Lt SHORT issued 1056A and 1056Ax	JMC
17	2/Lt ATKINSON joined from Base issued 480Bx	JMC
18	issued 1056A and 1056Ax Capt WILKINSON joined. Duke of Town Major ARKAS Capt MILNE dinner Commands. Issued 1124x. 2/Lt BROWN and 2/Lt MONSON posted to 159 and 157 Bdes.	JMC JMC
19	Issued 7FA	JMC
20	No Change	JMC
21	R.Q.C BERRY-SR joined from Base. Pans-Loos	JMC
22	Issued 0.91A+ issued 1130 B x	JMC

Army Form C. 2118.

WAR DIARY
INTELLIGENCE SUMMARY.
(Erase heading not required.)

January 1917

Hour, Date, Place	Summary of Events and Information	Remarks and references to Appendices
WANQUETIN 23	No 2 Sec. marched from BOURET. Capt CLOSMA	MO
K 32 C	2nd in Command East Town Major ARRAS	
SIGNS	Capt. WILKINSON took on duties of adjutant	
	after HAROLD joined with A+	
24	2/Lt Adjt BARNETT goes on leave	R/L
	His place is taken by 2/Lt G. SAMUEL	
	2/Lt Brown 158 Brigade	R/L
25	Nothing to report	R/L
26	— " — Issued 367 Bx	R/L
27	— " —	R/L
28	— " —	R/L
29	2/Lt PRICE proceeded on leave	R/L
30	Nothing to report	R/L
31	— " — issued nil	R/L

Army Form C. 2118.

WAR DIARY
~~INTELLIGENCE SUMMARY~~
(Erase heading not required.)

Instructions regarding War Diaries and Intelligence Summaries are contained in F. S. Regs., Part II. and the Staff Manual respectively. Title Pages will be prepared in manuscript.

Vol 13

Confidential

War Diary
30 D.a.C.
Feb 1st – February 1917
(Volume 13)

Place	Date	Hour	Summary of Events and Information	Remarks and references to Appendices

WAR DIARY
or
INTELLIGENCE SUMMARY
(Erase heading not required.)

Army Form C. 2118.

February 1917

Place	Date Feb	Hour	Summary of Events and Information	Remarks and references to Appendices
WANQUETIN	1		Issued 364 13X	
K.32.C	2		No change	
STENE	3		Issued 171A. Divisional Sgn altered. Lt LEWIS and Lt ATKINSON joined 50th Bde R.F.A. Lt TURNER posted to 9th D.A.E.	
	4		Issued 1000 RX	
REBREUVIETTE	5		Column left WANQUETIN 10.30AM arrived REBREUVIETTE at 2.25pm (via HAUTEVILLE. AVESNES. ETREE-WAMIN) Road slippery	
M.G. Central Shot SIC	6		No change	
	7		No change	
OUTREBOIS	8		Column left REBREUVIETTE at 8.15am arrived OUTREBOIS at 1.15pm (via REBREUVE - BOUQEMASON - DOULLENS - OCCOCHES) Roads bad	

Army Form C. 2118.

WAR DIARY
or
INTELLIGENCE SUMMARY
(Erase heading not required.)

February 1917

Place	Date	Hour	Summary of Events and Information	Remarks and references to Appendices
OUTREBOIS	9		Column left OUTREBOIS at 9.30 am. Arrived BOURDON 4.30 pm	OMR
BOURDON	10		via BERNAVILLE – BERNEUIL – DOMART – FLIXECOURT. Roads very	OMR
	11		Bad and Slippery. Billeted at DOMART, Lt BARNETT returned Rouen(?)	OMR
			No change	OMR
	12		Training commenced in Rot(?) Coys	OMR
	13		No change	OMR
	14		No change	OMR
	15		No change	OMR
			No change	OMR
	16		Lt Col A.H. BERLY handed over Command and went to U.K.	OMR
			No change	OMR

Army Form C. 2118.

WAR DIARY
or
INTELLIGENCE SUMMARY
(Erase heading not required.)

February 1917

Place	Date	Hour	Summary of Events and Information	Remarks and references to Appendices
BOURDON	17		Lt R. J. O'CONNOR and Lt R. MERCIER report for duty. Lt BANAN reported to Brigade to Rosieres to Staff Duty for duty.	
	18		Column left BOURDON at 7:30 am, arrived ARGOEUVES 12 noon (via ST-SAUVIER) Roads very deep and muddy	
ARGOEUVES				
AUBIGNY	19		Column left ARGOEUVES 7:45 am arrived AUBIGNY at 11:45 am (via LONGPRÉ – AMIENS – VEQUEMONT) Roads fair but very muddy.	
	20		Column left AUBIGNY at 9 am arrived HANGARD 12:30 pm (via FOUILLOY – VILLERS – BRETONNEUX – AUBERCOURT) Roads in a very bad state, our Mech Transport unable at points. A Inf & 13 Bn Sig Section found to take on to Hangard.	
HANGARD	20			
	21		Column left HANGARD 10:20 am arrived IGNAUCOURT 11:15 am (via AUBERCOURT) Roads very heavy from BERLY	
IGNAUCOURT				
V.27.B.7.9			Mechanical Transport arrived Bn H.Q. 3:44 A 13:38 A X	
ROSIERES				

Army Form C. 2118.

WAR DIARY
or
INTELLIGENCE SUMMARY

(Erase heading not required.)

February 1917

Instructions regarding War Diaries and Intelligence Summaries are contained in F.S. Regs., Part II. and the Staff Manual respectively. Title Pages will be prepared in manuscript.

Place	Date FEB	Hour	Summary of Events and Information	Remarks and references to Appendices
IGNAUCOURT	22		Signal 2297 A + 1578 A + 1108 B x	
V.27.B.7.S. ROSIERES Combles Ruf	23		2 Lt. A. Richardson posted to 157 Bde. Signal 1292 A x	
	24		Signal 760 A 1598 A + 834 B x	
	25		Nil	Signal 1718 A + 837 B x	
	26		Signal 304 A + 480 B x	
	27		Signal 1086 A 627 A + 142 B x	
	28		Signal 1368 A	

Army Form C. 2118.

WAR DIARY
or
INTELLIGENCE SUMMARY
(Erase heading not required.)

Vol 14

Confidential
War Diary
35 Bg. R.A.C.
From March 1 — March 31st 1917
(Volume 14)

Wilford LtCol
Comdg 35 Bde

Army Form C. 2118.

WAR DIARY
INTELLIGENCE SUMMARY
(Erase heading not required.)

March 1917

Place	Date 1917 MAR	Hour	Summary of Events and Information	Remarks and references to Appendices
IGNAUCOURT	1		Issued 2696 A 800 Ax 129 Bx	A/y/B
V.17.b.7.S.	2		Issued 1824 A 760 Ax 192 13x	A/y/B
ROSIERES Gun Fired Sheet	3		Issued 1140 A 228 Ax 192 13x	A/y/B
	4		Issued 3344 A 684 Ax 192 13x. Fine day – hot.	A/y/B
	5		Issued 1380 A 304 Ax 192 13x. Heavy loss of prisoner	A/y/B
	6		Issued 304 A 76 Ax 288 13x. Charles, Lt. THREEFALL priv. Jos.	A/y/B
	7		Issued 696 A 434 Ax 288 13x. Dust day	A/y/B
	8		Issued 2000 A 500 Ax 768 13x. Hard hot.	A/y/B
	9		Issued All.	A/y/B
	10		Issued 304 A 30 Ax 330 Bx. Good day.	A/y/B

WAR DIARY
or
INTELLIGENCE SUMMARY

(Erase heading not required.)

Army Form C. 2118.

Month: March 1917

Place	Date 1917 MAR	Hour	Summary of Events and Information	Remarks and references to Appendices
I.G. NAUCOURT	11		Issued 760 A. 836 A× 384 B×. Fine day	A115
V.27.b.7.5.	12		Issued 1064 H. 152 A× 384 B3×. ADVS visited all awards. Fine XXX	A115
ROSIERES Combined Shit	13		Issued 854 H 2094× 384 6×. Dull day	A115
	14		Issue A 304 H. 684 A× 192 B×. Dull & wet	A115
	15		Issued 238 A 836 A× 489 B×. 2.Lt HEANEY returns from WANDSWORTH to duty. Two two Sections for Siege Mor. Horses of all other Batteries	A115
	16		Issued 1526 H 912 A× 576 B×. Dull day	A115
	17		Issued 1064 H 1084× 576 B×. Fine day	A115
CAIX	18		Column moved to CAIX via ROYEUX at 9 a.m.	A115
E. 3.	19		arriving 10:30 A.M. Salvaged from bursefrom pit 2280. 547 ATX B×	A115
			Issued Jul. Salvaged from Supply Dumps. ATX B× 3598 1607 3×	A115
	20		No 2 Section moved to CURCHY for attachment to 32nd D.A.S.	A115

WAR DIARY or INTELLIGENCE SUMMARY

Army Form C. 2118.

March 1917

Place	Date	Hour	Summary of Events and Information	Remarks and references to Appendices
CAIX E.5. ROSIERES SHEET	20		2/Lt. B.K. JACOT from Base. Salvaged H17× R× A17× B× 1063 300 5542 1351	OYB OYB OYB
	21		Salvaged	OYB
	22		No Change	OYB
	23		No Change	
	24		2/Lt F.H. IRWIN, 2/Lt F.W. WHITEHEAD, 2/Lt R.F. CRUTTENDEN, 2/Lt W. SLADE joined from Base. 2/Lt CRUTTENDEN & 2/Lt SLADE to Pozy B44. 2/Lt JACOT to Pozy B44. L1573 ×	OYB
	25		No Change	OYB
	26		No Change	OYB
	27		Salvaged from Pin pits 32nd Division 2978A 8884× 3312 B× Capt. Hitchison seconded from II Corps.	OYB

WAR DIARY
INTELLIGENCE SUMMARY
(Erase heading not required.)

Army Form C. 2118.

March 1917

Place	Date	Hour	Summary of Events and Information	Remarks and references to Appendices
CAIX E.3	28		Relayed from 32nd D.A. 6342A 29674x 16648x	OMC
ROSIERES SHEET	29		Small arm section of 101 & 2 Sections marched to HERLY	OMC
	30		Gun ammn. Lt. Section of No.1 Sec'n marched at 9 am to Pargny. 61st B.A.C at PARGNY	OMC
NESLE I.19 Sheet 66 0	31		Remainder of Column marched from CAIX and arrived at NESLE at 2.30 pm. B.Echelon attached at MANICOURT. 6 P. wagons sent B.C. attached to 61 D.A.C. & 70 P. wagons to 32 D.A.C	OMRoy R.A. OMRoy R.A. Comdt. 33 D.A.C

WAR DIARY
or
INTELLIGENCE SUMMARY

Army Form C. 2118

Confidential

War Diary of
35 F.A.B.C.
for April 1st – April 30th 1917
(Volume 15)

Vol/5

OM Carly L.a.
35

Army Form C. 2118

WAR DIARY
or
INTELLIGENCE SUMMARY
(Erase heading not required.)

APRIL 1917

Place	Date April	Hour	Summary of Events and Information	Remarks and references to Appendices
NESLE I.19 Sh.66D	1		Very wet and cold. No change	OMP
	2		The detached Sections of No 1, 2 & 3 Sectns moved from MANNICOURT to HERLY, who's better cellars. Very wet.	OMP
	3		Bomb Stores formed at DOUILLY. Cold day	OMP
	4		Lt M.G. JENKINS joined from BASE. Heavy Snow. All wagons 2/Lt D. HAWKIN " " " felting up Gun ammunition and SAA for 32nd and 61st Divisions	OMP OMP
	5		No change - fine day.	OMP
	6		No change	OMP
	7		Issued 2880 Bx to 32 ASP. Cold and wet.	OMP
	8		49 Reinforcements arrived from BASE. Capt J.F.M. WILKINSON sent to 115 H.B. for attachment	OMP

WAR DIARY
INTELLIGENCE SUMMARY
(Erase heading not required.)

Army Form C. 2118

APRIL 1917 II

Place	Date April	Hour	Summary of Events and Information	Remarks and references to Appendices
NESLE I.9 SHEET 66D	9		No change. Cold and wet	AM/B AM/B
	10		Heavy snow	AM/B
	11		Column (Hq. B.Echelon and SAA Section of A.Echelon) moved from NESLE at 1.00 p.m. and arrived at MONCHY-LAGACHE at 4.00 p.m. Officers lived in Canvas, men in Cellars. Heavy snow	AM/B
MONCHY-LAGACHE Y.18 Central Sheet 62C	12		700R DN 2655 A 1038 SAA 69181 3x 558 D 240 D x from 61st DAC. Issued 756 A 404 AY 576 B x 350 Dx. No 12 Station and Park B.Echelon 61st DAC were attached to 35th DAC. No 2 Section 35th DAC remained with 32nd Division	AM/B
	13		Issued 486 A A 1292 A+ 576 B+ 179 Dx 2/Lt Short posted to 157 Bde. 2/Lt Irwin posted to 159 Bde.	AM/B

Army Form C. 2118.

WAR DIARY
or
INTELLIGENCE SUMMARY

(Erase heading not required.)

APRIL 1917 II

Place	Date	Hour	Summary of Events and Information	Remarks and references to Appendices
MONCHY-LAGACHE I.19 SHEET 66D	14		Issued 4472 A 1348 Ax 1392 Bx 260 Dx 2/Lt PRICE posted to 157 Bde. 2/Lt HEAVENS ~~TREWMAN~~ posted from RFA 157 Bde to DAC. fine day.	OMP
	15		Issued 1976 A 608 Ax 1188 Bx. Very wet	OMP
	16		Issued 2356 A 1216 Ax 192 Bx. Cold day	OMP
	17		Issued 1216 A 684 Ax 96 Bx 360 D 2/Lt IRWIN posted to 159 Bde. 2/Lt WHITEHEAD from DAC to 159 Bde	OMP
	18		Issued 380 Ax 192 Bx. Wet day. 15 Lynxheed of Wymount Coy permanently attached to each Infantry	OMP
	19		Issued 684 A 228 Ax 384 Bx All ammunition in dump Brigade Hdqrs. Sorted out into lots of the separate fuses.	OMP
	20		Issued 532 A 228 Ax. fine day	OMP

WAR DIARY
INTELLIGENCE SUMMARY

(Erase heading not required.)

Army Form C. 2118

APRIL 1917

Place	Date April	Hour	Summary of Events and Information	Remarks and references to Appendices
MONCHY-LAGACHE I.19 SHEET 66D	21		Issued 1292 A. 684 A+ 672 B+. Capt Milne attached to "N" Anti Aircraft Battery & O'Connor took over temporary command of No1 Section. Fine day	(M)AP
	22		Issued 1664 A. 684 A+ 432 B+. Fine day	(M)AP
	23		Issued 760 A. 836 A+ 96 B+. Fine day	(M)AP
	24		Issued 912 A. 304 A+ 1008 B+. Fine day	(M)AP
	25		Issued 298 A. 3052 A+. 576 B+ All sections and HQ moved away from the vicinity of Arras. Fine day	(M)AP
	26		Issued 1444 A. 532 A+ 576 B+. 2/LTH NOBLE joined from 40 Div.	(M)AP
	27		Issued 456 A. 152 A+ 134 B+.	(M)AP

WAR DIARY or INTELLIGENCE SUMMARY

Army Form C. 2118

APRIL 1917

Place	Date April	Hour	Summary of Events and Information	Remarks and references to Appendices
MONCHY-LAGACHE I.19	28		Issued 1216A 1444A× 288 B× 2/Lt HAWKIN to hospital with accidental wound in arm	
SHEET 66D	29		Issued 1444A 1140 A× 288 13×. 19 Drivers + 12 Gunners arrived from Base. Fine day	
	30		Issued 884 A 912 A+ 576 13× 2/Lt CAMPBELL joined from 61st Div. 38 R and 31 Div & posted to Brigade during the month, and received B 32 R & 61 Division also	

Army Form C. 2118

WAR DIARY
INTELLIGENCE SUMMARY
(Erase heading not required.)

Confidential

War Diary
of
35th M.G.Coy.

From May 1st — May 31st 1917
(Volume 16)

Reference to
1st Column of 35th [Coy]

Vol 16

Army Form C. 2118.

WAR DIARY
or
INTELLIGENCE SUMMARY
(Erase heading not required.)

MAY 1917

Place	Date May	Hour	Summary of Events and Information	Remarks and references to Appendices
MONCHY-LAGACHE N.E. 18 C.l. 2 SHEET 62.B	1		Issued 836 Ax. Lt JENKINS admitted to Hospital.	MB
	2		Issued 76A. 684Ax. 144Bx. Reinforcements from Base 12 drivers 6 Runners. 1 Saddler.	MB
	3		Issued 228A. 532Ax. Lt J.S.SMITH joined us from 157 Bde.	MB
	4		Issued 228A. 1368Ax. Dump was handed to new position owing to the danger of cellars being mined.	MB
	5		Issued 304A 760Ax 240Bx. Lt INGRAM and Lt CHAMBERS proceded on leave to UK. Lt CAMPBELL joined from 61st DAC	MB
	6		Issued 1444A. 2052Ax. 432Bx	MB
	7		Issued 912A. 1064Ax. Reinforcements to Bolton 32 drivers	MB
	8		No.1 Sec 61st DAC moved and were attached 32nd DAC No.II Sec 35th DAC rejoined from 32nd DAC. Issued 76A 76Ax 576Bx	MB
	9		Issued 556A 311Ax	MB

WAR DIARY
INTELLIGENCE SUMMARY

MAY 1917 II

Army Form C. 2118.

Place	Date May	Hour	Summary of Events and Information	Remarks and references to Appendices
MONCHY - LAGACHE IV. 19.	10		Issued 152 A 1064 Ax 886 Bx	APB
	11		" 1628 A 872 Ax 866 Bx	APB
SHEET 66.D. 62.C.	12		" 76 A 152 Ax	APB
	13		" 272 A 492 Ax. 28 Reinforcements arrived. Rev. E. W. de Normanville posted to DAC.	APB
	14		Issued 528 A. 380 Ax. General W.C. Staveley CB visited the lines. Dump.	APB
	15		" 152 A 988 Ax. "	APB
	16		" 228 A 532 Ax 3216 Bx. Capt. Smith went on leave to UK.	APB
	17		Reinforcements sent to Batteries 14. Returned to Corps Park 523 4A 342 Ax 2616 Bx. 61st DAC 4 and 6 Att attached to 35th Div. Lt Chambers returned from leave.	APB
	18		Returned to Park 2420 A 294 Ax 38 Bx	APB

SHEET 66.D. 62.C.

WAR DIARY or INTELLIGENCE SUMMARY

Army Form C. 2118.

MAY 1917

Place	Date MAY	Hour	Summary of Events and Information	Remarks and references to Appendices
MONCHY-LAGACHE Y 10 Cent.	19		Issued 76A . 675A× 288 B×.	
	20		" 76A 76A× . Returned to PARK 2072A 840 B×	
SHEET 66A 62C	21		Returned to PARK 1104A 1254 B×	
	22		Issued 100A 134 A×	
DOINGT 23 I 36	23		Column marched from MONCHY-LAGACHE at 7:00 am. Arrived 9:50 am. 24 Reinforcements arrived from BASE	
SHEET 62C	24		Column left DOINGT at 7:00 am and Marched to NURLU. Arriving at 10:00 am. No.1 Section new and at DOINGT to be attached 59th Div. 2t.A.G.I.CAMPBELL admitted to hospital	
NURLU D 16 a 62C	25		Lt.Col.BERRY proceeds to UK on leave. Capt CROXALL in command of Column.	

Army Form C. 2118.

WAR DIARY
or
INTELLIGENCE SUMMARY

(Erase heading not required.)

MAY 1917   IV

Instructions regarding War Diaries and Intelligence Summaries are contained in F. S. Regs., Part II. and the Staff Manual respectively. Title Pages will be prepared in manuscript.

Place	Date MAY	Hour	Summary of Events and Information	Remarks and references to Appendices
NURLU D.16.a 6.20	26		Bn's for WO STAVELEY visited New dump.	
	27		Issued 124 & 13 A×	
	28		2/Lt BUDD joined from BASE. Received 22 Reinforcements	
	29		Issued 152 A. 152 A×	
	30		Issued 178A. 152 A×. Capt SMITH and LINGHAM do from Rom leave. Capt SMITH took over Command of DAC	
	31		Issued 304 A×	

[signature]
Lt Col Commanding
35th ? DAC

WAR DIARY

INTELLIGENCE SUMMARY

Army Form C. 2118.

Confidential

War Diary
35 D.A.C.
From June 1st to June 30th 1917
(Volume 17)

Vol 17

Appendices
October 1917
Comdt 35 D.A.C.

Army Form C. 2118.

WAR DIARY
~~INTELLIGENCE~~ SUMMARY.
(Erase heading not required.)

Instructions regarding War Diaries and Intelligence Summaries are contained in F.S. Regs., Part II. and the Staff Manual respectively. Title pages will be prepared in manuscript.

June 1917

I

Hour, Date, Place	Summary of Events and Information	Remarks and references to Appendices
NURLU June 1.	Issued 76A 76Ax 96Bx. Fine day	MB
D16a	Issued 96Bx Capt MILNE holds to fourth AA Group.	MB
62e 3.	Issued 52A 152Ax 384 Bx. CRA visited Re dump.	MB
4.	Issued 228 Ax. CRA inspected New site to dump	MB
5.	Issued 228 A+. Started work on new dump	MB
6.	Issued 152 A	MB
7.	No change	MB
8.	"	MB
9.	"	Manmetz...?

WAR DIARY
INTELLIGENCE SUMMARY.
(Erase heading not required.)

Army Form C. 2118.

June 1917

Hour, Date, Place		Summary of Events and Information	Remarks and references to Appendices
NO R2U	June 10	Issued 96 Bx	
D16a	11	No change	
62c	12	Lt-Col BERLY returned from leave on 11/6/17. Issued 144 B3x. Lt W BARNETT leave to PARIS	
	13	Issued 76A 76Ax 96Bx. 2Lt W.G. NOAKES joined to DAC from BASE. Corps Horse Masterships adviser rockets the DAC	CMB
	14	Issued 152Ax 96Bx	CMB
	15	Issued 228A 608A 9613x	CMB
	16	Issued 96Bx	CMB
	17	Issued 152Ax 96Bx	CMB
	18	No change	

WAR DIARY or INTELLIGENCE SUMMARY

Army Form C. 2118

June 1917

Place	Date	Hour	Summary of Events and Information	Remarks and references to Appendices
NURLU D16-a 62C	19		Issued 96 Bx. 152 Ax. Lt L W BARNETT returned from leave to PARIS.	OWA
	20		Issued 152A. 152Ax. 96 Bx	OWA
	21		Issued 142 Ax. 48 Bx. 2Lt NOAKES posted to 159 Bde. 2Lt BEAVAN joined on first Commission	OWA
	22		Lt INGLIS proceeded on leave to U.K.	OWA
	23		Issued 76 A+ 96 Bx. Survey Party started at NURLU and Tanks to New Site.	OWA
	24		Issued 38A 380 Ax 96 Bx	OWA
	25		Issued 192 Bx	OWA
	26		Issued 152A 144 Bx	OWA
	27		Issued 96 Bx. Lt HEANEY returned to Dae from TOWN MAJOR BOUES.	OWA

Army Form C. 2118.

WAR DIARY
INTELLIGENCE SUMMARY.
(Erase heading not required.)

June 1917

Place	Date	Hour	Summary of Events and Information	Remarks and references to Appendices
NURLU	28		Issued 152 A X	Orders
D 16 a That 62 a	29		Issued 152 A 152 AX 96 BX	Orders
	30		In charge. Reinforcements during month of June 20 O.R. Arrived from Base 4 N.E. 261 O.R. Posted to Bdes	WB Ingham Captain WB Ingham Captain Comdg.

WAR DIARY
INTELLIGENCE SUMMARY.
(Erase heading not required.)

Army Form C. 2118.

Vol 18

Confidential

War Diary
of
35 D.A.C.

From July 1st to Feby 21st 1917
(Volume 18)

Army Form C. 2118.

WAR DIARY

INTELLIGENCE SUMMARY

(Erase heading not required.)

JULY 1917. I

Instructions regarding War Diaries and Intelligence Summaries are contained in F. S. Regs., Part II. and the Staff Manual respectively. Title pages will be prepared in manuscript.

Place	Date 1917 July	Hour	Summary of Events and Information	Remarks and references to Appendices
NURLU	1		Issued 404 A 584 Ax 96 Bx	AF B
D.16.a	2		Hauled OR Ammunition dump at HEUDICOURT to 40th DAC	AF B
62.C.	3		No 2 Section attached to 40th DAC	AF B / AF B
	4		Lt INGLIS returned from leave.	AF B
	5		No Change	AF B
	6		"	AF B
	7		" No 2 Sec returned from attachment	AF B
K.13.b			Column left NURLU at 1.15 pm. Arrived HAMEL 3.15 pm	AF B
62.C	8		No 1 Section of 59th DAC attached for duty to the Column	AF B
	9		Issued 144 Bx 176 A 176 Ax 48 Bx	AF B / AF B

Army Form C. 2118.

WAR DIARY
or
INTELLIGENCE SUMMARY.
(Erase heading not required.)

JULY 1917 II

Instructions regarding War Diaries and Intelligence Summaries are contained in F. S. Regs., Part II. and the Staff Manual respectively. Title pages will be prepared in manuscript.

Place	Date 1917 July	Hour	Summary of Events and Information	Remarks and references to Appendices
HAMEL K.13.b.	10		No 1 Sec. 59th DAC attached for duty. Issued 176A 176Ax 48 Bx	AH/B
62C.	11		1032A 932Ax 2648x	AH/B
	12		668A 820Ax Lt HEANEY and Lt JENKINS proceeded on leave 576 Bx	AH/B AH/B
	13		200A 200Ax 576 Bx	AH/B
	14		1064A 608Ax 288 Bx	AH/B
	15		152A 108Ax Capt WILKINSON proceeded on leave	AH/B
	16		304Ax	AH/B
	17		76A 76Ax. CRA Brig Gen. WC STAVELEY visited the Camp. Maj Gen FRANKS. GOC 35th Div visited Camp	AH/B

Army Form C. 2118.

WAR DIARY
or
INTELLIGENCE SUMMARY.

(Erase heading not required.)

JULY 1917

III

Place	Date	Hour	Summary of Events and Information	Remarks and references to Appendices
K.13.b.b2.c.	18		Issued 152Ax. 2/Lt BUDD transferred to R.F.6. 2/Lt F.R SMITH noted from 159 Bde, Arrived in hospital	
	19		Issued 96A 96Ax	O.K.B O.K.B
	20		Issued 380A 228Ax 288Bx 2/Lt CAMPBELL went on leave	O.K.B O.K.B
	21		" 48Bx	O.K.B
	22		" 228A 380Ax 480Bx. Column Sports held. Maj. Gen FRANKS the GOC Div, and Brig. Gen. STAVELEY the CRA attended	O.K.B O.K.B
	23		Issued 288Bx	O.K.B
	24		" 152A 192Bx Lt GOODWAY wounded in action	O.K.B

Army Form C. 2118.

WAR DIARY
INTELLIGENCE SUMMARY.
(Erase heading not required.)

JULY 1917

IV

Place	Date 1917 July	Hour	Summary of Events and Information	Remarks and references to Appendices
K.13.b	25		Issued 50A 50Ax 242 Rx	OMB
62.C	26	"	4348A 228Ax 132Ax(Smoke) 1368 Rx	
			Capt WILKINSON returned from leave, and took over Command	OMB
			of No 1 Section Lt. O'CONNOR proceeded on leave	
	27		Issued 4520A 818Ax 500Ax (Smoke) 1296 Rx	OMB
	28	"	27A 31Ax 306 Rx Capt CROXALL proceeded on leave	OMB
	29		No change	OMB
	30		Issued 228Ax 480 Rx	OMB
	31	"	238A.	OMB

Reinforcements for Month From Base 50
To Bases. 20 } Reinforcements from BASE 33

Army Form C. 2118.

WAR DIARY
INTELLIGENCE SUMMARY
(Erase heading not required.)

Vol 19

Confidential

War Diary
of
35th D.A.C.
from 1st — 31st August 1917.
(Volume 19)

Army Form C. 2118.

WAR DIARY
or
INTELLIGENCE SUMMARY
(Erase heading not required.)

Instructions regarding War Diaries and Intelligence Summaries are contained in F.S. Regs., Part II. and the Staff Manual respectively. Title Pages will be prepared in manuscript.

August 1917

Place	Date 1917	Hour	Summary of Events and Information	Remarks and references to Appendices
MARWAIX K.13.b SHEET 62.9	Aug 1		Wet day. Issued Nil. Teams out on fatigue 63	MPS
	2		Dull day. No 2 Sec. 59th DAC joined for attachment. No 1 Sec 59th DAC left to join 34th Division. 2/Lt A.G.J. CAMPBELL returned from leave. Teams out. 59	MPS
	3		Dull day. Issued nil. Teams out 59	MPS
	4		No change. Issued 96 Bx. Teams out 55	MPS
	5		Fine day. " 126 AX. 120 AX. Teams out 68	MPS
	6		Very wet. " 804 A 424 AX. 384 Bx. No 1 Sec 59th DAC Coy back for attachment. No 2 Sec 59th DAC joined 34th Div. Teams out 77	MPS
	7		Wet day. Issued 576A 272AX 144 Bx. Lt Col A.H. BERLY went to Hospital. Capt J.F.M. WILKINSON assumed Command. Capt F. adjt Teams out 79	Marwaix Command Capt F adjt

Army Form C. 2118.

WAR DIARY
or
INTELLIGENCE SUMMARY
(Erase heading not required.)

Instructions regarding War Diaries and Intelligence Summaries are contained in F. S. Regs., Part II. and the Staff Manual respectively. Title Pages will be prepared in manuscript.

August 1917 II

Place	Date	Hour	Summary of Events and Information	Remarks and references to Appendices
MARQUAIX K.13.b SHEET 62g	AUG 1917 8		Fine day. Issued 684 A. 912 Ax. 336 Bx. 2/Lt R.J.O'CONNOR returned from leave to U.K. Jeans ont 82	MB
	9		Wet day. Issued 760 A. 304 Ax. 240 Bx. Jeans ont 78	MB
	10		Wet day " 456 A. 152 Ax. 144 Bx. 900 B.Sx. " " 73	MB
	11		Dull day " 608 A. 304 Ax. 384 Bx. Capt CROXALL	
			Returned from leave to U.K. 2/Lt F.J.PREWITT Joined from BASE. Jeans ont 87.	MB
	12		Fine day. Issued 258 A. 1748 Ax. 1392 Bx. 896 N. Jeans ont 150	MB
	13		" " " 2672 A. 3782 Ax. 418 Ax (Smoke) 840 Bx. 904 N. 692 Nx. 2/Lt F.R.SMITH Struck off Strength Rejoined in ENGLAND. Jeans ont - 154	[signature] Captain

WAR DIARY or INTELLIGENCE SUMMARY

Army Form C. 2118.

August 1917

Place	Date	Hour	Summary of Events and Information	Remarks and references to Appendices
MARQUAY K13.b	AUG 1917 14		Fine day. Issued 4400 A. 2688 Ax. 700 Ax (Smoke) 576 Bx. 4408 N. 2520 MK Jeans out 111	
SHEET 62.C	15		Dull day. Issued 602A 468Ax 282A(Smoke) 100N. DADVS wished all animals. Jeans out 66	
	16		Wet day. Issued 456A 608Ax 576 Bx 600Ax (Smoke) 69 2" MTM SO 2"TM Jeans out 92	
	17		Fine Day " 304A. 456Ax. 480Bx. 550 PxShura. 10 B&K SO 2"TM Jeans out 82	
	18		Fine day " 682A. 398Ax. 1529Ax Shura. 48Bx Shura 680Bx 176H 100MK Jeans out 55	
	19		Fine day " 667A. 6714 Ax. 4550 Bx. 96 Bx Shura. 4654 Jeans out 132	

WAR DIARY
or
INTELLIGENCE SUMMARY

(Erase heading not required.)

Army Form C. 2118.

August 1917 IV

Place	Date 1917	Hour	Summary of Events and Information	Remarks and references to Appendices
MARQUAY	20		Foggy dull day. Issued 464A. 4012 Ax. 2576 Bx. 360 Ax Smoke 206 Ax Shore 50.2" TM. Tear - out 104	
K.13.b				
SHEET 62.c.	21		Fine day. Issued 2052 A. 1440 Ax. 63c Bx. 800 N Bosox Tear - out 81	
	22		" 304 A. 228 Ax. 1150 Bx. Camp Shelters. Inf 24 rounds 210 m/m HV shell four hits on huts on Lines of Hts	
			3 Section No damage done. Tear - out 89	
	23		Fine day. No 3 Section moves to New Camp at LIÈRMONT. Issued 988 A. 1272 Ax. 1152 Bx. 30 B Thermite. Lt B.W. INGRAM struck off strength (accident) Tear - out 84	
	24		Fine day. A Echelon moved to New Camp at LIÈRMONT. Issued 228 A. 152 Ax. Tear - out 74	

Army Form C. 2118.

WAR DIARY
or
INTELLIGENCE SUMMARY

(Erase heading not required.)

August 1917

Place	Date	Hour	Summary of Events and Information	Remarks and references to Appendices
MARQUAIX K.13.b SHEET 62.C	25		Fine day. Issued 2660 A. 1292 Ax. 1752 Bx. 100 9us. 100 2"TM Teams out &c	
	26		Rained later. Lt Col A.H. BERLY Started off Sheepeth (15. F. D) Scot on ENGLAND. Lt Col D.E. FORMAN O.N.G. Assumed Command. Issued Nil. [crossed out] Transport.	B57
HERAMONT D.12.d SHEET 62.c	27		Head Quarters moved to HÉRAMONT. Transport 71. Blowing a gale in morning. Heavy rain commenced about midday & continued all night	B57
	28		Issued 228 A. 228 Ax. 96 Bx (4LYN. 1358 Nx. Returned to DAC) 100 2" TM. 509 us. 18 G.S. Wagons, Coms f, 6 M.K.2 Mule teams and 1 Cart Mattes in K.3 Ams. Returned to a draft of HT Depot on reorganisation of D.A.C. Jennings.	B57
	29		Rained at intervals; fine morning Wet day. Issued m f 34. Issued 304 A. 304 Ax (934 M 934 N+ Returned to Parc)	B57

WAR DIARY
or
INTELLIGENCE SUMMARY

(Erase heading not required.)

Army Form C. 2118.

August 1917 VI

Place	Date 1917	Hour	Summary of Events and Information	Remarks and references to Appendices
HERAMONT D.12.d SHEET 62.c	30		Issued 738A. 706A+ 144 B+. Lt B W INGRAM posted to DAC from Hospital. Rained all day. Issued nt & 3 Btt.	
	31		Issued 277.6A. 2016.A+. 2306 B+. 100 2"TM Wet day. Jean S. on't 50. Gale abating by degrees, but heavy rain at intervals. moved all horses into the village, onto line outside. [illegible crossed-out lines]	B. Johnson - Lieutenant

Army Form C. 2118.

WAR DIARY
~~or~~
INTELLIGENCE SUMMARY
(Erase heading not required.)

Instructions regarding War Diaries and Intelligence Summaries are contained in F. S. Regs., Part II. and the Staff Manual respectively. Title Pages will be prepared in manuscript.

Place	Date	Hour	Summary of Events and Information	Remarks and references to Appendices

Vol 20

Confidential

War Diary
of
35th M.T of A.C
From 1st — 30th September 1917
(Volume 20)

WAR DIARY
INTELLIGENCE SUMMARY
(Erase heading not required.)

Army Form C. 2118

SEPTEMBER 1917

Place	Date 1917	Hour	Summary of Events and Information	Remarks and references to Appendices
LIERAMONT D12.d SHEET 62.c	Sept 1		Dull day. No rain. Ammunition issued Nil. On representations of C.O. the Column has been one month's complete rest from fatigues, in order that the men and horses may recuperate. Ammun issued nil	MB
	2		Dull day. Issued from A.R.P. 650 Bx. 608 N. 724 Nx.	MB
	3		Fine day. 2 Lt J.F. KING posted from 159 Bde. Issued 226A. 152Ax.	MB
	4		Fine day. A.D.V.S. III Corps inspected all animals in the Column. Issued Nil.	MB
	5		Fine day. C.R.A. visited the Column. 10 M. III Corps visited the Column re: repair of wagons. Issued 15 Bx 9.45 T.M	MB
	6		Fine day, but heavy shower later. Issued nil	MB
	7		Dull foggy day - fine later. Issued nil	MB
	8		Dull foggy day - fine later. 66 RDAx Smoke. 10 Px. km.	MB
				B Journey from Col

WAR DIARY
or
INTELLIGENCE SUMMARY

(Erase heading not required.)

Army Form C. 2118.

SEPTEMBER 1917

Place	Date 1917	Hour	Summary of Events and Information	Remarks and references to Appendices
LIERAMONT	9		Beautiful day. Issued N.L. LIERAMONT EMPIRE was completed and opening show given by Divisional Concert Party.	MB
D.12.d.	10		Revd. STAVELEY was present.	MB
SHEET 62c.	11		Splendid day. Issued 110 Bx.	MB
			Very fine day. Issued 190 Bx. Concert given at night by local talent.	MB
	12		Dry day but very strong wind. Issued nil. Boxing Exhibition in LIERAMONT EMPIRE versus 159 Bde. D.A.C won 4 matches to 1.	MB
	13		Fine day. Capt. L.W. BARNETT went on leave to U.K. Issued 96 Bx	MB
	14		Dull day. Strong wind. M.G.R.A. IIID Army inspected the animals and reported 18 too light and 13 too heavy for L.D. and 74 in fair condition and in need of a rest. Concert at night by Cheshire Concert Party.	MB
	15		Dull and showery day. Advisor on Horsemanship to IIID Corps	MB

Army Form C. 2118

WAR DIARY
or
INTELLIGENCE SUMMARY

SEPTEMBER 1917

III

(Erase heading not required.)

Instructions regarding War Diaries and Intelligence Summaries are contained in F. S. Regs., Part II. and the Staff Manual respectively. Title Pages will be prepared in manuscript.

Place	Date 1917	Hour	Summary of Events and Information	Remarks and references to Appendices
MERAMONT	Sept 15	Continued	inspected all animals. D.D.R.W. Specked animals classified as unfit for Artillery work. Issued Nil	MB
D. 12. d SHEET 62C	16		fine day. Issued 152 A.	MB
	17		fine day. Issued 295 A. 2t J.S. Smith went on leave to U.K.	MB
	18		fine day. Issued Nil	MB
	19		fine day. Issued 309 + 5 T.M.	MB
	20		fine day. Issued Nil. Great rain at night	MB
	21		fine day. Issued 192 Bx	MB
	22		fine day. Issued Nil. B.A. & Cap.8. III Corps. Pu HAMBRO visited the Column. Boxing Competition D.A.C. v 157 Bde D.A.C. Won. 4 matches to 1	MB

B. Stewart
Major

WAR DIARY or INTELLIGENCE SUMMARY

Army Form C. 2118

SEPTEMBER 1917 No. IV

Place	Date	Hour	Summary of Events and Information	Remarks and references to Appendices
LIGRAMONT D.12.d SHEET 62.C	23		Fine day. Issued 76A. 152Ax. 449 Bx. Observers party sent to New Camp at BUIRE to prepare it for move	MB
	24		Fine day. Turn out inspection of No 2 and 3 Sections, Brig Gen. W.C. STAVELEY present. Issued 192 Bx	MB
	25		Fine day. Turn out inspection of No 1 Section. Brig Gen W.C. STAVELEY present. Issued 152 At	MB
	26		Fine day. Capt BARNETT returned from leave. Issued 152A. 384 Bx.	MB
	27		Fine day. Issued 76A. 76Ax.	MB
	28		Fine day. Maj Gen FRANKS (Comdg 35th Divn) visited Camp and inspected horses	MB
	29		Fine day. A Sub SAA Section marched out with 104 Sup Bde to PERONNE on way to ARRAS SECTOR. Issued 76A. 152x	MB

WAR DIARY or INTELLIGENCE SUMMARY

SEPTEMBER 1917

Army Form C. 2118.

Place	Date	Hour	Summary of Events and Information	Remarks and references to Appendices
LIÉRAMONT D.12.d SHEET 62.C	30		Fine day. Issued 228 AX. B. Browning Lieut Col. Commdg 35th D.A.C.	

Army Form C. 2118.

WAR DIARY
INTELLIGENCE SUMMARY
(Erase heading not required.)

Vol 21

Confidential

War Diary
of
35th D.A.C.

Nov 1st – 31st October 1917
(Volume 21)

B. Strawbenzie
Lt Col
Commdg 35th D.A.C.

Place	Date	Hour	Summary of Events and Information	Remarks and references to Appendices

Army Form C. 2118.

WAR DIARY
or
INTELLIGENCE SUMMARY

(Erase heading not required.)

OCTOBER 1917

Instructions regarding War Diaries and Intelligence Summaries are contained in F. S. Regs., Part II. and the Staff Manual respectively. Title Pages will be prepared in manuscript.

Place	Date OCT	Hour	Summary of Events and Information	Remarks and references to Appendices
LIERAMONT D.12.d	1		Fine day. B Sub Section of S.a.a. Section marched out to ARRAS Sector with 105 Inf. Bde. Issued 15TMK 152A 176AX 324BX.	
62.C.	2		Fine day. Col. LAMBART of the 55th DAE, who were taking our form no came over and looked round Camp. A Echelon filled up with ammn preparatory to move. Issued 1584 A. 528 AX. 322 BX	
	3		Dull day. Lt PREWETT proceeded on leave. C Sub Section of S.a.a. marched out with 106 Inf Bde. Issued 3142A. 1034 AX. 600BX	
	4		Dull and showery. HQ – No 1 and No 2 Sections marched from LIERAMONT at 10 am and arrived at BUIRE 12.30 PM, distance about 9 miles – good roads. All personnel in bell tents. Heavy rain during night and very cold.	
BUIRE J.32.a. 62.C	5		Dull and showery. Wind shifted round towards N about noon. Hard storm during afternoon followed by pronounced drop in temperature. Store lines very muddy and have to be shifted frequently.	

Army Form C. 2118.

WAR DIARY
or
INTELLIGENCE SUMMARY

(Erase heading not required.)

OCTOBER 1917

Place	Date Oct	Hour	Summary of Events and Information	Remarks and references to Appendices
BUIRE J.32 a 62. C	6		Projected scheme of systematic progressive training during the rest of the Ine" period seems to be in the bad weather. Movement of vehicles away from the roads would end the animals. Bitterly cold in early morning with sharp frost. High bomb and shorts during the day.	MJJ
	7		Clocks put back to ordinary time during the night. Lts G.S. SMITH and CHAMBERS returned from leave and horsemanship course. Continuance of cold and showery weather but both men and animals are standing it well. Horse line chaufed to fresh ton ground ground second day.	MJJ
	8		Very cold wet day. All officers and men recalled from leave.	MJJ
	9		Lt. INGLIS reported to O from S.A.A. Section an ARRAS tractor, reports Sgt. Section far more comfortable than the rest of Columns by the men and most of the Animals being in billets. Cold Stormy weather continues. GOC of Division - Rev. FRANKS - wishes to the DAC in the morning, was very complimentary on the condition of the horses	MJJ

WAR DIARY

INTELLIGENCE SUMMARY

OCTOBER 1917

Army Form C. 2118.

Place	Date	Hour	Summary of Events and Information	Remarks and references to Appendices
BUIRE J32a G.C.	9		Lt O'CONNOR granted special leave to U.K.	
	10		Fine cold wet morning but finer in afternoon. Col FORMAN borrowed a car from IIIrd CORPS and visited the 3 Lefratis Inspection of the 30a Section in billets at DAINVILLE – DUISANS – MANIN respectively. All 3 were much better housed than we are at H.Q. and are having a completely peaceful time (Lt INGLIS reported S.a.a. section the first night without rain since our arrival at BUIRE.)	
	11		Fine day. Lt PREWETT returned from leave (recalled). A Substitutes compass race for 35th DA was held today for prize presented by Pew FRANKS (Comdy Div) Pew STAVELEY (B.G.R.A.) and Col DAVSON (Comdr. 159 Bde). 13 pairs started. All 3 prizes won by 35th DAC. Draft of 20 men arrived from Base. Heavy rain during night.	
	12		Advanced party under Lt INGRAM left to take over new area in XIV Corps area	

Army Form C. 2118.

WAR DIARY
INTELLIGENCE SUMMARY

OCTOBER 1917

(Erase heading not required.)

Instructions regarding War Diaries and Intelligence Summaries are contained in F.S. Regs., Part II. and the Staff Manual respectively. Title Pages will be prepared in manuscript.

Place	Date Oct	Hour	Summary of Events and Information	Remarks and references to Appendices
BUIRE J.32.C 62.C	12		Heavy rain all night. Movement of Division to join 5th Army commenced today	
	13		Blew a gale all day but no rain	
	14		First fine day for a long time. Marched by road to PERRONNE as will. HQ 7:30 No 1, 9:10 No 2, 11:20 and took Entrainments at 2:10 p.m. HQ all loaded in train in 1½ hours. Arrangements at ABBEVILLE were bad, water for men too hot, cold and the train went in front to enable the train up. Arrived PROVEN 11:30 a.m. via AMIENS - ABBEVILLE - ETAPLES - BOULOGNE - ST OMER - HAZEBROUCK. Detrained in 2 hours. Cars sent for Mess in Lorry lorries Lutero and fell and moved off at 7:00 a.m. Camp is a fine hill full of sticky holes and difficult about out but East of ELVERDINGHE. No 2 (Arr? Arrived at 3:30 p.m. for PROVEN, and No 1 Sec at 5:30 p.m. Raining Marched from ESQUELBECQ. Heavy for Nothing has led and lost	
	15			

WAR DIARY
or
INTELLIGENCE SUMMARY

Army Form C. 2118.

OCTOBER 1917

Place	Date	Hour	Summary of Events and Information	Remarks and references to Appendices
Near ELVERDINGHE B.16.a. Sheet 28	Oct 16		Dull day, but no rain. L.M.C. ourselves into Camp. Few shells and shorts landed up to right of B'ers. pitchwise a great bunch. Col Forman reconnoitred the country East of Canal. 2/Lt PREWETT and 9 men took over the Bomb store from the friends and 17th Divn. A.V.M. Stopped shot which seems a lot of boots to get into shape.	
	17		Heavy rain during night. Lt MERCER went on leave. Sea destroyers marched in today and camped alongside No 2 bc at WHITEHYPE. Corner B.10.d. Four bombs dropped in S.E.A. at 5pm, one right in the camp but only one horse wounded which had to be destroyed later.	
	18		Took over 3 A.R.P.'s wh. 20,000 odd rounds of ammn. 1800 rounds of 18 fdr ammunition up to Battery position. Order to carry on the WIJDENDRIFT Road about five miles from the A.P. started to Divn. in this. Fine day, many S.A. over at different times during day.	

WAR DIARY
or
INTELLIGENCE SUMMARY

Army Form C. 2118.

OCTOBER 1917

Place	Date	Hour	Summary of Events and Information	Remarks and references to Appendices
Near ELVERDINGHE B.16.a Sheet 28	18		S.O.C. Section moved into our new and permanent Camp on the ELVERDINGHE – POPERINGHE Road B.18.b. We was quite a fair field and necessitated a lot of work to make it anything tolerably as the section was supplying batteries to fire about 20 Pl 4in guns for R.E. Continued all night firing up ammunition to guns. 3 O.F. & King Gun	
	19		Bright day. Gas war. So shoop on the WIDDENBRIEK road that No lorry to Sevice. The tanks been and fired 5 ammunition was. Wires which were subsequently destroyed by shell fire. Foggy day – Rival storm in afternoon. Ammunition following well faces only traffic carried on all day. Roads nearly shell and the Dugout Chambers on ad at BOESINGHE & STEENBEEK rendered unsafe. Pack Convoys managed to get through. Col FORMAN inspected ? to STEENBEEK with military police any man partly through out. Death freely included attack of road shragles together. Can Mrs B(?) Lt O'CONNOR retimed from leave.	B.Browning Lt

WAR DIARY or INTELLIGENCE SUMMARY

Army Form C. 2118.

OCTOBER 1917

Place	Date	Hour	Summary of Events and Information	Remarks and references to Appendices
War ELVERDINGHE B.K.6	20		Fine day. Sent out pack animals with ammunition at the usual time. These proved to be the only successful method. Passed ammunition all day. Believed we have 6500 rounds which were taken from the place where we had to dump it the previous day. Believe in the 3 days 11,500 rounds carried.	
			Wounded 2 horses killed 2 R.S. [?] Sent below with 2 Heavy Sections to collect [?] wire for the Infantry. These were embers taking up ammunition back to batteries to get on [?]	
	21		Fine day. 10 RS wagons in afternoon to daily 20 sent up with R.E. Material. No ammunition packed. Roads heavily shelled and the S.S. hopers had a bad time getting through. H.Q. and Section 1,2,3 moved into tent event Camp at B.13 a 5,6, taken over from 20th Day. Some mules stay out the night and must get the Corses clothe too far from the road.	
	22		Fine day. Packing continued to the same. Believed fire/1ism on the STEENBEEK Casualties 20 R. wounded. 2 horses killed and 2 wounded.	

WAR DIARY
INTELLIGENCE SUMMARY

Army Form C. 2118.

OCTOBER 1917   VIII

Place	Date	Hour	Summary of Events and Information	Remarks and references to Appendices
ELVERDINGHE B.13.a.	Oct 23		At B.W INGRAM proceeded on leave. Dull day with some rain. Shelled 800 Ry to 159 Bn, an F.O.O. Bx dump & W.& R. position on Arasmite & Kavan Shelling the 20 PR heavies had a bad time getting through as enemy were concentrating fire on the Corps roads. Casualties 2 OR wounded 4 Rank & file killed and 1 wounded.	(illegible signature)
	24		Fine morning, rained later. Orders to Capt to start a New A.R.P. South of canal at WOLVERTON B.6.d.2.6. — So new Rd forward and work commenced. Sig Slack L.O. Continuous relief of Chell. undo. Secured DPS Troops of RE attached to WIDDENDRIFT by 157 Coy & no 3 & 29/157 Casualties 2 OR wounded, 4 Ranks killed, 2 OS bulges w/nd wounded including Capt (illegible)	(illegible signature)
	25		Very high wind all day. Much drifted at night and bright moon. Many Ram A/c bombing between 8 pm — 11 pm. Flying Unit for Park up DPS down L to the two Bns. All available PSwagons Pack up to New A.R.P. Casualties 2 OR wounded, 1 Horse killed, 3 R.J.OCONNOR sent to Base under GRO 1384. 2/Lt F.A.IRWIN to full Ambulance (NYDN)	(illegible signatures)

2449 Wt. W14957/M90 750,000 1/16 J.B.C. & A. Forms/C.2118/12.

Army Form C. 2118.

WAR DIARY
or
INTELLIGENCE SUMMARY

(Erase heading not required.)

OCTOBER 1917

Place	Date	Hour	Summary of Events and Information	Remarks and references to Appendices
SAME PLACE	26		Rained all day. No ammunition available at dumps. Salvage and delivered 200 Bx to B/157. Wiring New A.R.P. progressing well.	JMO
	27		Fine day. Packed 1240 A and 456 Bx to the 2 Bdes. Casualties 1 knee killed. E.A. over at night from dump. One bomb fell in a field in No 2 Section lines killing 2 mules and wounding 1. Several S. shells and bombs fell around A.R.P. at Marron and the Bourt Store but did no damage. 2Lt D.W.H. Johnson returned from hospital.	JMO
	28		Dull but no rain. Packed 604 Bx and 300 A to Batteries. Bdes. Lieut Stewart, 7 Fromelles and Fanconberg Rds- now por dump L.D.	AJPG
	29		Fine day. Cloudy. C.R. packed 760 A and 550 Bx to Batteries. 7 E.A. over about 11 p.m., two bombs near our lines but no casualties. All S.S. before Fanconberg Rd. material.	Burners Woning JMO
	30		Very wet and cold. Packed 320 A 9400 Bx to Bdes. Casualty 1 O.R. wounded	

2449 Wt. W14957/M90 750,000 1/16 J.B.C. & A. Forms/C.2118/12.

Army Form C. 2118.

WAR DIARY
or
INTELLIGENCE SUMMARY

(Erase heading not required.)

Army Form C. 2118.

Month and Year: OCTOBER 1917

Place	Date	Hour	Summary of Events and Information	Remarks and references to Appendices
SAME PLACE	30 Cont.		E.A. over about 2am in any found dropped four falling in our lines killing 7 and wounding 27 Civilians also, one R.F. horse also destroyed. No casualties to men.	[sig]
	31		Fine day. Packed 16440 A and 5208x. All F.d. Ur fires out for R.E.	[sig]
			Ammunition delivered issued to various units by A.R.P. from 18th – 31st [sig]	
			A Ax Bx Lethals Total	
			71,926 23,797 29,778 7,345 132,846	

[signatures]

Vol 92

WAR DIARY
OF
INTELLIGENCE SUMMARY.

Confidential

War Diary
of
35th D.A.C.
June 1st – 30th November 1917
(Volume 22)

WAR DIARY
INTELLIGENCE SUMMARY

Army Form C. 2118.

NOVEMBER 1917

Place	Date	Hour	Summary of Events and Information	Remarks and references to Appendices
ELVERDINGHE	Nov 1 1917		Very dull day - no rain. Am Packed up 1120 18pdr and 560 Bx to Bdes. No 1 Pit fab. prs.	AMB
B.13.a	2		Dull day - no rain. Delivered 584 18pdr and 596 Bx to Batteries. (all Salvage ammunition) Commenced Salvage operations, turning up all Dud Shell to Batteries.	AMB
	3		Dull day - clouds v. low. Delivered 576 18 Pdr to Batteries. Several men passed but remained with unit. Gen. FRANKS inspected Camp and was very complimentary on appearance of men and animals.	AMB
	4		Cloudy morning - fine afternoon. 576 18 pdr and 14 Bx to Batteries. Capt. WILKINSON sent to FRENCH CORPS as Cps Artillery Liaison officer. 209 damaged 18 Pdr Shells to SOLFERINO FARM Salvage dump.	AMB
	5		Dull day - no rain. Genl MADDOCKS the new CRA inspected Camp. No fatigues, on a lot of work putting Camp up the Cp.	AMB

D. D. & L., London, E.C.
(A8004) Wt. W1771/M2 31 750,000 5/17 **Sch. 53** Forms/C2118/14

Army Form C. 2118.

WAR DIARY
INTELLIGENCE SUMMARY.
(Erase heading not required.)

NOVEMBER 1917

Place	Date	Hour	Summary of Events and Information	Remarks and references to Appendices
Hoist	6		2nd Lieut Paul & CHAMBERS went on leave. 2nd Lieut E. Hahnant left for our Salvage Dump Rutly cart lift Cses.	AHB
ELVERDINGHE				
B.13.a	7		Just Morning Drew in afternoon 15 GC wagons with ammunition lifts setup of dumps.	AHB
	8		Cold and cloudy. Capt BARNETT detailed to Div HQ for wear of guns W. of PROVEN for two divisional artilleries. Usual De Fragts.	AHB
	9		Cloudy day showery at night 21 wagons Refilling Ammunition Went on leave.	AHB
	10		Heavy rain. Col FORMAN arranged for salvage all ammunition etc to keep Cow ab our STEENBECK on the Dumb in front. All officers went up to Reconnoitre area Roberts.	AHB

Army Form C. 2118.

WAR DIARY
or
INTELLIGENCE SUMMARY.

(Erase heading not required.)

NOVEMBER 1917

Instructions regarding War Diaries and Intelligence Summaries are contained in F. S. Regs., Part II. and the Staff Manual respectively. Title pages will be prepared in manuscript.

Place	Date	Hour	Summary of Events and Information	Remarks and references to Appendices
Moat	Nov 1917 11		Heavy rain, clearing at night. Lt Threefall returned from hospital	M/13
ELVERDINGHE	12		Fine day. Capt BARNETT injured. Salvage parties out. Sgt BEVING awarded the Military Medal for gallant conduct with Lewis Gun.	M/14
B.13.6.	13		Fine day. Salvage operations continued. APD of 2nd Lancs Fus. Shelter with about 20 Damels to 8" HV. Also hit & great ard one Rifleman wounded. Road, damaged about 30 feet ft of Homme Nb Dock 32 bricks wounded from shrapnel.	M/5
	14		Fine day. Gas shell later vicinity of APD of M Pillbox L. 4.3.2. No damage. 100 R over book site at POND COTTAGE C.14.c.8.2. also poor shown with L.G. and all rifle fire was too far. M/s Lt. (T/C) HALLS awarded the Military Medal for patrol	

WAR DIARY
or
INTELLIGENCE SUMMARY.

Army Form C. 2118.

NOVEMBER 1917

Place	Date	Hour	Summary of Events and Information	Remarks and references to Appendices
	15		Fine day. School Pres. Intr'd Cam for fm term of Class open from 1 – 3	
ELVERDINGHE			all & not Eggts our Camp & REPN TRENCHES Returned to Camp at 5	
B.12.a	16		MERGER Bath to 157 Bde	MR
			Fine day Patrols Continued	MA
	17		do	MA
	18		do No 2 Coy moved into Fort Hoover opposite	MB
			Fine day. Convoy flour (? ord ?) by 28th PAS	
	19		Lt COL DEPORATH left on leave & Lt MADDOCKS took over cmd	MB
			2 O.R. and 2 mules wounded whilst down Salvage	
	20		Lieut REV. A. INGRAM to hospital with Influenza	

Army Form C. 2118.

WAR DIARY
or
INTELLIGENCE SUMMARY.
(Erase heading not required.)

NOVEMBER 1917

Place	Date	Hour	Summary of Events and Information	Remarks and references to Appendices
[Neuf?]	21		Dull day. Snow. Saw 1/CHAMBERS returned from leave. [illegible]	MS
EAVERDINGHE	22		Dull day. Snow. Saw Palace continued.	MS
B.15.a	23		Fine day. 1/T INGLIS went on leave. Many Eamour shower day and night. No limits of spots close.	MS
	24		Very high winds. But saw few MADDOCKS called. Palace continued.	MS
	25		Very high wind and cold. Palace continued. Casualties 3 OR killed Gunner L. KIRK 50[?] R.F.A. shot. Ref. [illegible] front trench.	MS
	26		About [illegible] and a very cold [illegible] [signature] to OC	

Army Form C. 2118.

WAR DIARY
INTELLIGENCE SUMMARY.   NOVEMBER 1917
(Erase heading not required.)

Place	Date 1917	Hour	Summary of Events and Information	Remarks and references to Appendices
Mar	Nov 27		High wind & front. Our Cav. made obsv. Harbour Camp, etc.	
ELVERDINGHE			Fired 4 rounds from Four 6" NAVALS. Railhead and wharfage S/6.	
A.B.a	28		WOALAERTON. Capt. SMITH returned from leave.	
			High wind, mid-rain. Continued obsv. as yesterday. Patrols active at...	
	29		Fine day, high wind. E.a. on at night. No fronts on our line. H.A.	
			firing found steady throughout night, No shells hit our camp	
	30		Fine day. Patrols active. Shell by H.A. few rounds	
			108 H.Hs. - 2 rounds. 3 german hangars hit. 3 Hos Sunes	
			Eagles trying for front for march. 3 Couns high velo. 110,000 Empty bath	
			Service no 1. chemical shops. Guernmenttes 18 pdr shraps. cases.	
			18 Pdr HOW Chemical	
			23569 8822 1795 1303 10,026 293	

Army Form C. 2118.

WAR DIARY
INTELLIGENCE SUMMARY.
(Erase heading not required.)

SECRET

Vol 23

35th Divisional Ammunition Column.

From 1st December 1917
To 31st December 1917

Volume 23.

B. Forrester
Lieut Colonel
Comdg 35th D.A.C.

Army Form C. 2118.

WAR DIARY
INTELLIGENCE SUMMARY.
(Erase heading not required.)

DECEMBER 1917

Instructions regarding War Diaries and Intelligence Summaries are contained in F.S. Regs., Part II. and the Staff Manual respectively. Title pages will be prepared in manuscript.

Place	Date	Hour	Summary of Events and Information	Remarks and references to Appendices
Near ELVERDINGHE B.13.a Sheet 27	1st		Strong wind some rain. Not taking ammunition. Capt. G.J. ABBOTT awarded the Croix-de-Guerre by the Sir Commanding II French Corps for gallantry in doing the line. Delivered 8376 rounds to Battries.	
	2nd		Sergt Huns & Cpl Salvage took photo. Kents Hunts & Harris (67 joined Hand Base) Hf huts erected on Palat to Elverdinghe this date. Delivered 3416 rounds of ammn.	
	3rd		The day very cold. Many E.A. planes over during night 10 bombs dropped near our Salvage operation continued. Delivered 2644 rds to Batteries. 1101 rounds of thirteenth Amm. 197 " " Valenceph Amm — The day very cold & little snow fell during afternoon.	
	4th		C.R.A called to inspect stores, work to Relieve to Elverdinghe tents to Battries which were replaced in the evening by huts. Having decided to replace all L.D. tents by L.D. huts	

Army Form C. 2118.

WAR DIARY
INTELLIGENCE SUMMARY. December 1917

(Erase heading not required.)

Instructions regarding War Diaries and Intelligence Summaries are contained in F. S. Regs., Part II. and the Staff Manual respectively. Title pages will be prepared in manuscript.

Place	Date 1917	Hour	Summary of Events and Information	Remarks and references to Appendices
Near ELVERDINGHE B13a Sheet 27	Dec 5		Fine clear day. Very frosty. Salvage operations continued & heavy fatigues for batteries. E.A. planes over several times during the night. No bombs dropped in our camp. N/K Gorman returned from leave. (Eng land) (5400 rounds of Ammn delivered)	JR
—	6th		Fine day. Hard frost. Salvage continued — 20 waggons R.E. fatigues. Delivered 2350 rounds Ammn.	JR
—	7th		Frost broke, quick melt. Salvage operations continued. G.O.C. Heavy took over as look out over camp	JR
—	8th		Fine day. Salvage operations continued. 16th Divn. relieved on our front. Coys detailed ready for move. Bomb dropt landing field 5.15 P.M. by K? Bombs. Comments very complimentary on work of Lieut Prewett & party at Bomb Stors. 885 rounds of 13 pr 88 & ammunition delivered during week. 136 rounds 9 Howitzer	JR / —

B. Gorman
Lieut & Q.M.
Comdg 35 D.A.C.

2353 Wt. W2544/1454 700,000 5/15 D. D. & L.   A.D.S.S./Forms/C. 2118.

WAR DIARY
or
INTELLIGENCE SUMMARY

Army Form C. 2118.

December 1917

Place	Date	Hour	Summary of Events and Information	Remarks and references to Appendices
Near ELVERDINGHE B.13.a Sheet 27.	Dec 9 1917		Revd. A.F.T.P. handed over to 57th D.A.C. Lieut Inglis returned from leave & 1/Lt. Capt Withrow rejoined from Ludlow duty with II Tank Corps. Strength nil B. n 2 1/Lo. 57 S.A.B.	JL
E.10d.78. Sheet 27.	10th		Column marched to HAANDEKOT REST AREA, moved off at 8.30 a.m. and arrived at camp about noon. Distance travelled about 12 miles. Very good roads. Weather fine, troops cheery. Men mostly billeted in Sheds & Barns. Good quarters for nearly whole of Bde. Horse picketed in postern land. Standings had been started at horse of the Bdes. Very hard during day.	JL
	11th		Fine day, a little rain. Capt. Ashton Bond, attached to R.A.S.G. for Course of Instruction, Lieuts Dukes, Lieut Rogers returned to duty. Regrd Admn no. in absence of Capt Barnett. During the absence of Capt Barnett Lieut Jardine Parker Assumes D.A.S.S	JL

WAR DIARY or INTELLIGENCE SUMMARY

Army Form C. 2118. DECEMBER 1917

Place	Date	Hour	Summary of Events and Information	Remarks and references to Appendices
E10d7.8- sheet 27	Dec 1917	11½	To atturne the raid & wait the party of Captain her day publication in foreign papers. 20 re-improvements carried from Rale	
	12"		do do "15th" Lieut. (now) Jones for duty.	
		10am	The class Roy. No 13289 Sgt. J. W. HENDERSON M.M. be awarded MILITARY MEDAL for gallantry near Hargicourt. The Divisional Commander Major Gen. FETTIGREWS pulled men return to A Co. of wh. the following att. F. Sgt. (second ribbon colour)	
			Corpl. ABBOTT Croix de Guerre Sgt. HENDERSON MILITARY MEDAL	
			Received orders to march to 2nd Corps Rest area & the neighbourhood of ARNEKE	

B. Symes
Lieut.
Comdg 105

WAR DIARY or INTELLIGENCE SUMMARY

Army Form C. 2118.

December 1917

Place	Date 1917	Hour	Summary of Events and Information	Remarks and references to Appendices
ARNEKE AREA H18C Central Sheet 27	Dec 13th		Bgd. marched to ARNEKE via HERZEELE via HOUTKERQUE - HERZEELE - WORMHOUDT - ESQUELBECQ distance about 15 miles along good road. Very long Col. Cavalry marched off. I.train arrived at Herzeele about 7pm. Officers then billeted. Good accommodation for Officers & horses had to move these officers to have been in reserve before was everything was clean & front. Headquarters established at H18C Central. About 27 Weeks Supply Sent 15 O.R. posted to Brigade joint towards made road to Bayeul Lieut Lanaud ……… Vade road to Bayeul. 9th O.R. arrived from Calais where he stayed there 20 days whilst there he wrote to General Asquith & Marshal & always to Clothier. Then Training.	[signature] D. Townsend Comd 13rd

WAR DIARY
INTELLIGENCE SUMMARY

Army Form C. 2118.

December 1917

VI

Place	Date	Hour	Summary of Events and Information	Remarks and references to Appendices
ARNEKE PRET H.18.c Central Sheet 27	Dec 1917 /14		Fine day. Attention is now chiefly of the Royal Artillery. The following changes to "LANCE" Bombardier being charged to "LANCE" Bombardier. 24 O.R. posted to Brigade. C.O. inspected the billets & lines of sections (now) very very comfortable & happy & they all look fine. The rest were the appreciated by all ranks after the strenuous time of the past two months.	
	15		C.O. & day. Lt Col Inman to C.R.S. Capt Nicholls assumes command of the Column.	
	16		13 O.R. posted to the Bde. Divine Service for all ranks & morning. Freemans NCO pleased in Command of the day.	Lieutenant Colonel 36 DAC

W. T. Lesting
Lt Col

WAR DIARY of INTELLIGENCE SUMMARY

Army Form C. 2118.

(Erase heading not required.)

Place	Date 1917	Hour	Summary of Events and Information	Remarks and references to Appendices
	17		Light rain. Usual camp training in accordance with programme submitted to B.G. Lieut Inglis (Gunner) & dispatch (armourer) have Dec 14 1917.	
	18		Lieut Webster joined from Base goes to ride. Party of 1 officer & 20 O.R. proceeded by rail to collect remounts (mules) for Base duty Column. (Showery all day. Training on going)	
			77 mules arrived & distributed to section 24 Horse L.D. posted to 157 Bde RA. 39 " " " 159 Bde RA.	
	19		Weather mild. Training continues.	
	20		Weather mild. A party of 1 officer & 40 O.R. proceeded to British Army Salvage Works at Calais left with two 6 ten[?] trucks to ass[?] in salvage returns.	

WAR DIARY December 1917

INTELLIGENCE SUMMARY

Army Form C. 2118.

Place	Date	Hour	Summary of Events and Information	Remarks and references to Appendices
	Dec 1917 21		Very cold, heavy frost during night. 7 bombs fired by Lieut (Sergt KIRBY) The 133 R.C.I. (Corp. the first). The R.A.B. be expected to operate with compensatory stopping the sounds.	R
	22		Heavy very high traces (ratten correct to state of ground) Pte SHIVES A. No 1 Sect discharged to commission. Lieut Johnson granted 21 days not leave in England. Orders received for C.Y.E. R.C. I.N.C. & ranging station -	R
	23		Afternoon. Chief frosty. Stan front Carl fordson (Screed) a line to U.K. all ranks busy preparing for Xmas	R
	24		Xmas day - gun was to finish if the whole of those clear. Snow most extensive. Xmas fare & were hors d'oeuvre fresh pork of Xmas & Xmas pudding. Reinforcement arrived about 5pm dating tea in club for 8 days. Sent them to billets at once	R
	25			R

FRNEXE AREA
H 18 c central Sht 27

WAR DIARY or INTELLIGENCE SUMMARY

Army Form C. 2118.

December 1917

IX

Place	Date	Hour	Summary of Events and Information	Remarks and references to Appendices
HRNEKE AREA	Dec 1917 26		Foggy. Kept us day to training possible.	
	27		Snowing. A party of Officers & 12 Others paid a visit to Some Rear Communication Partys. Others and [illegible] at Dunkerque at the invitation of the R.A.F. Our trip was made easier by the map reading competition for Officers & N.C.O's held [illegible] & [illegible] places won by one N.C. Lieut Havington & Sergt [illegible] & [illegible]. [illegible] pairs to 15th [illegible]. B & [illegible] sectors carried and the Division. 6 of the [illegible] is taken [illegible] by the R.A.F. [illegible].	
			Stoky this Capt McKenzie returned from [illegible]. 2 (Acting Capt) [illegible] [illegible] to UK as officers attached. A lecture by an Officer of the R.A.F. on the history arms of that Branch of the Service.	

Army Form C. 2118.

WAR DIARY
of
INTELLIGENCE SUMMARY. December 1917

(Erase heading not required.)

Instructions regarding War Diaries and Intelligence Summaries are contained in F. S. Regs., Part II. and the Staff Manual respectively. Title pages will be prepared in manuscript.

Place	Date	Hour	Summary of Events and Information	Remarks and references to Appendices
	29/12		Musketry shaw to be completion of Musketry - Demo. under competition history)	
			1. Best turned of Team & Armed Mayn.	
			N° 1 Lct. team gaining 1st place	
			N° 3 Lct. 2nd place	
			Teams were inspected by Maj Gen Bushrook Kelly	
			Adviser to H Army. He was highly complimentary in Turnout	
			2. Inter Cos Lewis Gun N°1 Team of "D" Coy	
			in final.	
			3. Musketry Completed - 2nd Team gaining 1st place	
			Lekang returned from leave & U.K. & took over Sergt	
			Drummer off M.L. Beaver.	

WAR DIARY
INTELLIGENCE SUMMARY. December 1917

Army Form C. 2118.

Place	Date	Hour	Summary of Events and Information	Remarks and references to Appendices
ARNEKE AREA H18 c central (about)	30 1917		Light thaw. 36 G. Wagons. Team wheels on thin ducks ie 20 to Corps Supply Column 10 to B.A.O. drome 6 " Divisional Pack service	
			B.A.C. teams now available on three hrs. notice in readiness. Slight thaw rag - frosty at night. ADS. commanded (but ?) Inspected the B.A.C. officials satisfaction with acts he saw. Small match in D.C. football Crushers played Mobile team lost 1-0 to A/157.	AR [signature] AR [signature] B. Armour. Colonel. Wim ? D.A.C. Comdg 35 D.A.C.
	31			

Army Form C. 2118.

WAR DIARY
or
INTELLIGENCE SUMMARY.
(Erase heading not required.)

Vol 24

SECRET

35TH DIVISIONAL AMMUNITION COLUMN.

From 1st JANUARY 1918.
To 31st JANUARY 1918.

VOLUME. 24.

James T Armour Capt
Acting/Cmdg. 35. D.A.C.

Instructions regarding War Diaries and Intelligence Summaries are contained in F. S. Regs., Part II. and the Staff Manual respectively. Title pages will be prepared in manuscript.

Place	Date	Hour	Summary of Events and Information	Remarks and references to Appendices

WAR DIARY
INTELLIGENCE SUMMARY. January 1918

Army Form C. 2118.

Instructions regarding War Diaries and Intelligence Summaries are contained in F.S. Regs., Part II. and the Staff Manual respectively. Title pages will be prepared in manuscript.

(Erase heading not required.)

Place	Date	Hour	Summary of Events and Information	Remarks and references to Appendices
Osnelle H.18.6.4/6 Sheet 27	1-1-18	—	Frosty early morn. Snow during day. L/Cpl FORMAN returned from 6. C.S.	89H
"	2	—	Rapid thaw during day. Frost during night	89H
"	3	—	Snow during morning. Freezing during day. Remount party proceed to Chaptuzat to collect 16 mules (52) 21 Horses posted to Bdes. 52 O.R. reinforcements join from Base 32 Cent direct to L. Bde. 18 retained at B.A. Col. 24 mules arrive from 37th D.A. Col., 2 more O.Rs to B.U.P. NH+2 FBROUCH	89H
"	4	—	Freezing. B.C. visits teams in Thaw precautions 28 mules arrive from No 4 Fla Renfrew Lecture Pts JOHNSON and HARDY return from leave 2nd Lieut Omond y Handy at C.O. 35th D.A. Bde.	89H

(A8604) D. D. & L., London, E.C. Wt. W1771/Ma 31 750,000 5/17 Sch. 53 Forms/C2118/14

Army Form C. 2118

WAR DIARY
or
INTELLIGENCE SUMMARY.
(Erase heading not required.)

January 1918

Instructions regarding War Diaries and Intelligence Summaries are contained in F. S. Regs., Part II. and the Staff Manual respectively. Title pages will be prepared in manuscript.

Place	Date	Hour	Summary of Events and Information	Remarks and references to Appendices
Armentières H.18 C.4-6 Sheet- 2 y	5.1	—	Thaw during morn, C.O. inspected animals that arrived previous day. They are a poor lot.	89F
	6"	—	Heavy frost during night. C.R.A. inspected mules which arrived from 4th Army F. Ram Sec² & 37.O.A.6	89F
	7"		Heavy thaw. All wagons turned out for puppy work	89F
	8"		Heavy snow storm. Roads bad. C.R.A. provided prizes for "Assault at Arms". 9.a.6. Prizes 1st & 2nd snap reading Comp². 1st. Turn out wagon 1st Wrestling on horseback. 1st F. W. Perring C.O. visited new area. Freezing hard during night	89F
	9"		Still freezing. F.A. C.M. 8	89F
				J.M.W. Hann, Capt. actg. C.O. 35" Bn. F. A. A.F.C.

D. D. & L., London, E.C. (A8004) Wt. W17711/M2 31 750,000 5/17 Sch. 52 Forms/C2118/14

Army Form C. 2118.

WAR DIARY
INTELLIGENCE SUMMARY
January 1918

(Erase heading not required.)

Instructions regarding War Diaries and Intelligence Summaries are contained in F.S. Regs., Part II. and the Staff Manual respectively. Title pages will be prepared in manuscript.

Place	Date	Hour	Summary of Events and Information	Remarks and references to Appendices
ANNEKE H.18 c.4.6. Sheet 27	10c		Bhaw. Q.A. C. moved to transfer area T.24.A.9.3 * T.24.B.8.6. Via ESQUELBEC, WORMHOUT, HERZEELE, HOUCKERKE, WATOU. going good, last picture arrived in camp 5 p.m. Camp fairly good, horses under cover, men in huts.	894
HANDHOEK T.24.A.Q.3 T.14.c.86.	11c		Snow now almost gone. As usual lectures also 6"8" Q.A.C. lines which we are taking over.	894
"	12c		Snow plight from Sentence of Dr Cooper (promulgated) 10 years P.S. Capt² Jenkins (894) Jenkins rejoined from leave.	894

J.M.W. [signature] O.M.
act. C.O. 35th Q.A. C.F.A.

Army Form C. 2118.

WAR DIARY
INTELLIGENCE SUMMARY.
(Erase heading not required.)

January 1918

Place	Date	Hour	Summary of Events and Information	Remarks and references to Appendices
HANDHUSK X24 a 9.3 X14 c 8.6	13		Marched to ELVERDINGHE AREA. Crews good moral. O.H at 8.30 A.M. all pickings & H.Q. in Camp by noon. 87	
"	14		Col. FORMAN 89th took over Temp command of 159 "Bde. Parties and fatigues took over duties in the line. 2/Lt. TRENMAN 89th 2/Lt. HARRING(?) 89th } party of 22 on salvage work 89th 21 G.S. Wagons on road work Heavy fall of snow during night. C/- CAMPBELL 89th from leave	
	15		Snow during morning. Storm during afternoon. 26 Teams & Wagons turn out on thaw precautions work	

J.M. Wittman Capt.
Act C.O. 35th Q.A.R.

ELVERDINGHE B 13 A 3.7

WAR DIARY
or
INTELLIGENCE SUMMARY.

Army Form C. 2118.

January 1919

(Erase heading not required.)

Place	Date	Hour	Summary of Events and Information	Remarks and references to Appendices
ELVERDINGHE B.13.a.3.1 Sheet 28	16th		Raining during fore-noon. Mild afternoon. 26 teams & wagons on Sham precaution work	89/4
	17th		Heavy gale. Snow & Rain. Labour operating 20 Wagons & teams on Sham precaution work	89/4
	18th		Mild day but trying. 2/Lt Smith proceeded on leave. 2/Lt Prenett 89/4 returned from bomb plane 2/Lt Johnson 89/4 took over bomb store	89/4 89/3
	19th		Mild & wet. Hostile planes flew over in evening 89/4. No bombs dropped in the vicinity of this camp. Maj: R.S. May visited Salvage area & the various dumps.	89/4

Armstrong Capt
Act: C.O. 35-9 a.b.c.

Army Form C. 2118.
V/1

WAR DIARY
or
INTELLIGENCE SUMMARY.
(Erase heading not required.)

January 1918

Instructions regarding War Diaries and Intelligence Summaries are contained in F. S. Regs., Part II. and the Staff Manual respectively. Title pages will be prepared in manuscript.

Place	Date	Hour	Summary of Events and Information	Remarks and references to Appendices
ELVERDIN(G) B.13.A.3.1 Sheet 28	20th		Day fine. Church Parade Service. General fatigue Salving & thaw precautions.	897
	21st		Dull. Thaw precautions cease. Take over 2nd Corps A.R.P. Buffs R.D from 32nd D.A to B2 (ARBUR-) [THRELFALL 891] Lieut Threlfall in charge. B2 (ARBUR-) fatigue parties Charge of Distributor Gas sheet dump.	897 897
	22nd		Dull. Rain. Lieut Ingram [INGLIS 30H] takes over A.R.P R2 [THRELFALL 891] from O/C Threlfall. Inspection of Camp by C.R.A.	897
	23rd		Bright. Adj. visited the various dumps. Usual Salving & General fatigue.	897

signed [signature] Major
a/c O.C. 135th A.R. Coy.

Army Form C. 2118.

WAR DIARY
INTELLIGENCE SUMMARY.
(Erase heading not required.)

JANUARY 1918   VII

Place	Date	Hour	Summary of Events and Information	Remarks and references to Appendices
ELVERDINGHE B.13.A.5.7 Sheet 28	24.1		Lieut CROSSLEY joined from Base. C.O. visited the various dumps & Salvage area. Usual Salving & fatigue.	894
	25		Fine. Salving work & Engineer fatigue. R.S. Maj. visited the various dumps. Usual Salving & General fatigue.	894
	26		Bright. Usual Salving & General fatigue.	894
	27		Heavy fog. Coy. visited Salvage area & various dumps. Usual routine Salvage & fatigue.	894

J.M.McIlwaine Capt.
act. O.C. 35th A. Coy.

WAR DIARY or INTELLIGENCE SUMMARY

Army Form C. 2118.

VIII

JANUARY 1918.

(Erase heading not required.)

Instructions regarding War Diaries and Intelligence Summaries are contained in F. S. Regs., Part II. and the Staff Manual respectively. Title pages will be prepared in manuscript.

Place	Date	Hour	Summary of Events and Information	Remarks and references to Appendices
ELVERDINGHE B.13.A.3.1. Sheet 28	28		Hard frost during night. Usual Salving & fatigue	894
	29		Salving and general fatigue parties during night.	894
	30		Frosty in morn thaw during day. Salving & road work	894
	31		Very hard frost. Fatigues for A.S. Coys. Salvage & general transport work.	894

O.C.A.H. BARNETT R.W.

Lieut Colonel & 10th W.R. proceeded on leave.

9 MMCArmour Capt
Act O.C. 35th D.a. B.

Army Form C. 2118.

Vol 25

WAR DIARY
or
INTELLIGENCE SUMMARY.
(Erase heading not required.)

35th Divisional Ammunition Column.

From: 1st February 1918
To: 28th February 1918

Volume 25.

SECRET.

Capt. R.F.A.
Comdg. 35th Div. Ammunition Column.

Place	Date	Hour	Summary of Events and Information	Remarks and references to Appendices

WAR DIARY or INTELLIGENCE SUMMARY.

Army Form C. 2118.

FEBRUARY 1918.

Instructions regarding War Diaries and Intelligence Summaries are contained in F. S. Regs., Part II. and the Staff Manual respectively. Title pages will be prepared in manuscript.

(Erase heading not required.)

Place: ELVERDINGHE BELGIUM Sheet 28 - B13 A97 TROUSSEL FARM

Date	Hour	Summary of Events and Information	Remarks and references to Appendices
1st		Salvage continued – 20 wagon employed. Went away for Cpl Ward a total of 46 G.S. and 15 L GS wagon out today. Corp'l Boorman i/c & proceeded to England for Cadet course.	H
2nd		Wash cart from Lieut INGLIS proceeded afresh. Lieut THRELFALL N. took over charge of Dump leave to England. N. continued. Total of 39 G.S. 9 L.G.S. wagon out. Salvage work continued. Labour with column 5a wagon G.S. & 9 L.S.S. Carserine Labour with column out.	H
3rd		Salvage continued. 3 Ceasure hand out for Corp Pyecroft sent. 28 Stores transferred to Rangate N. FORTINGTON N. Lichere accidentally killed (Thorn frm horse) Lt PEPER & Lt Smith returned from leave to U.K. 40 G.S. wagon & 5 L G.S wagon out.	H
4th		Salvage & Agricultural work continued Lt PEPER attained duties of Adjutant of Column a party of 1 NCO & 3 OR proceeded to Calais to collect remount 52 G.S wagon, 15 L.G.S. wagon out	H
5th		Salvage & Agricultural work continued 50 G wagon & 1 T. L.G.S. wagon out	H
6			H

D. D. & L., London, E.C.
(A8604) Wt. W1771/M2 31 750,000 5/17 Sch. 52 Forms/C2118/14

WAR DIARY
INTELLIGENCE SUMMARY. FEBRUARY 1918.

Army Form C. 2118.

Place: ELVERDINGHE BELGIUM (ROUSSEL FARM) Map Sheet 28 B.19.a.9.7

Date	Hour	Summary of Events and Information	Remarks
7		Salvage & Agricultural work continued. 33 O.R. & 2 N.C.O.s ORs. 15 O.R. arrived from Base.	
8		Salvage & Agricultural work continued. 3 Sgts & 2 L.G.S. ORs & 14 O.R. posted to Brigades. 7 O.R. proceeded on leave to U.K.	
9		Salvage & Agricultural work continued. 31 O.R. & 7 L.G.S. wagon out.	
10		Quartermaster Salvage & Agricultural work continued. 42 G.S. & 9 L. G.S. wagon out. Handed on HILL TOP & POND COTTAGE Road start to 1st Division. Took on BARDS CAUSEWAY Rock store.	
11		Salvage & Agricultural work continued. 44 G.S. 7 L.G.S. wagon out. Handed on BUFF ROAD R.P. 61st & took on WOLVERTON R.P. from 32nd Division.	
12		Salvage & Agricultural work continued. 44 L.G.S. 7 L.G.S. wagon out.	
13		Salvage & Agricultural work continued. Inspection of Column by BRIG. GEN. MADDOCKS, L.TH.BELFALL & 10 G.S. proceeded on leave to U.K. 4 4 G.S. & 9 L.G.S. wagon out.	

WAR DIARY of INTELLIGENCE SUMMARY

Army Form C. 2118.

FEBRUARY 1918

Place: High Chalk 26 B13a.2.1. ELVERDINGHE (BELGIUM) (ROUSSEL FARM)

Date	Hour	Summary of Events and Information	Remarks and references to Appendices
14		Salvage & Agricultural work continued, 4.3. G.L. & 7L.G.S. wagons at.	JR
15		Lieut. F.J. PREWETT posted to 7.P.14 & 7P.F.A. Base Depot. Formerly rept. for L.E. Salvage & Agricultural work continued. 4.6. L.L. & 7L.G.S. wagons at.	JR
16		50 O.R. reinforcement arrived for Batt. 2 officers & 4 N.C.O. proceed to ROUEN to draw URD's preparatory to arrival of Drafts. Proceeded to D.A.C. men to be attached. Salvage & Agricultural work continued 4.3. L.L. & 7L.G.S. wagons at.	JR
17		Lieut. HOLDER arrived from Base. Salvage & Agricultural work continued. 3.6. L.L. & 9.L.G.S. wagons at. Captain WILKINSON proceeded on leave to U.K. also 6 O.R. 50 O.R. posted to Brigade.	JR
18		Salvage & Agricultural work continued 3.5. L.L. & 10. L.G.S. wagons at. Captain BARNETT returned from leave. Relieved Command of the Column.	JR
19		Salvage & Agricultural work continued 4.6. L.L. & 13.L.G.S. wagons at.	JR
20		Salvage & Agricultural work continued 4.1. L.L. & 12.L.L. G.S. wagons at. 6 O.R. returned from leave. Chaplain Reverend proceeding class also 10 O.R. to Base.	JR

WAR DIARY or INTELLIGENCE SUMMARY

Army Form C. 2118.

Place: ELVERDINGHE (BELGIUM) (ROUSSEL FARM) Map Sheet 28 B 2.a.9

FEBRUARY 1918

Date	Hour	Summary of Events and Information	Remarks and references to Appendices
21st		Salvage & agricultural work continued. 3 O.R. + G.S. G.S. wagon at 2 Lt. H.F. PHILLIPS joined for duty from Brigade. 4 engineers from 17 Section of Brigade. Engineers from B Coy. to U.K. 1 Officer + 16 O.R. to Calais to collect horses & 13 O.R. proceeded on leave to U.K.	JR
22nd		Salvage & agricultural work continued. 3 E.R. + 10 C.S.L. wagon at 4 sixteen carts to Brigade. 18 L.D. horses + 6 mules posted to Brigade.	JR
23rd		Salvage & agricultural work continued. 3 Q.b. + 10 G.S. wagon at Bdm. H.E. SMITH M.I. duties ceased to Sergeant at own request.	JR
24th		Salvage & agricultural work continued. 4 O.R. + 11 L.G.S. wagon at M.G. Company. The Column (M Gen.) G.M. FRANKS C.B) inspected the Column & expressed his satisfaction at all he saw in every thing that a very fine spirit must exist in the Column to enable such a standard to be attained. 30 mules arrived from Calais – they part condition.	JR
25th		Salvage + agricultural work continued. 48 L.D. + 11 L.S. wagons at	JR

WAR DIARY or INTELLIGENCE SUMMARY

Army Form C. 2113.

FEBRUARY 1918

ELVERDINGHE (BELGIUM)
(ROUSSEL FARM)
Ref Sheet 28. B 13 c.1.

Place	Date	Hour	Summary of Events and Information	Remarks and references to Appendices
	26.		Salvage & Agricultural Volunteers). 52 OR & 2 C.S.M. Lagreed. 9 O.R. proceeded on leave to U.K.	JR
	27.		Salvage & Agricultural Vol. returned. 52 O.R. & 2 C.S.M. agreed. 2 Dinner Packs to D/157 Bde RFA.	JR
	28.		Salvage & Agricultural went (returned) 57 O.R. & 1 O.R. Glasgow out 15 O.R. from Rear. 2 N.C.Os for Gas Course Rest Specified as fit to be "Unit Gas N.C.Os." In addition to the daily Salvage & Agricultural work the Parties each of 1 Officer + 12 O.R. have been employed daily since the 16th of the month burying in positions for Corp. + Army Reserve positions. Attached (Appendix 1) is a statement always "Salvage" F.S.R.I. and above that solid by the Greece pay worthy under direct orders of the Staff Captain 35th D.A. Unit- & full Amounts of events is received here.	JR

WAR DIARY
INTELLIGENCE SUMMARY

Appendix I

FEBRUARY 1918

Army Form C. 2118.

ARTICLES SALVAGED between 15/1/18 and 28/2/18

AMMUNITION
- 34307 rounds S.A.A.
- 307 "
- 58 "
- 248 18 pounder shells
- 160 4.5" Charges
- 16170 empty S.A.A. cases
- 50 Very Lights
- 279 Grenades (various)
- 6 Hypo Pak
- HV picric clips

SHELTERS etc
- 61 Nissen Huts, Elephant Iron
- 102 type "C" Shelters
- 36 French Boom
- 22 Tomb C S L

CLOTHING
- 11 Jackets S.D.
- 17 Trousers
- 5 Great Coats
- 11½ pr Ankle Boots
- 7 Shirt Flannel
- 14 Linen
- 10 pr Worsted Drawers
- 1 Box respirators

MISCELLANEOUS
- 19 Wire Gauges
- 8 W.L.L. pins
- 4 Dicy Lstern
- 3 Pick Handles
- 9 Bivvy sheets
- 24 Curb clips
- 3 Angle Iron
- 24 Yds. Rubber
- 1 Reel cavity

MISCELLANEOUS
- 1 Pick Bag
- 3 War Stamp
- 5 cwt sling wire
- 2 Stamp R.O.
- 6 Rifle ammo
- 50 Yards Sisal rope
- 11 Green Sheets
- 7 Rifle M.L.E.
- 3 Browne Rifles
- Purfia
- 1 Knapsack Buckle
- 3 Cart Bivvys
- 263 Sir Arms Covers
- 44 Horse Rubs
- 1 Elephant Iron sheet (damaged)
- 1 motor pump
- 1000 H.O. hand grenades
- 49 rounds

Army Form C. 2118.

WAR DIARY
or
INTELLIGENCE SUMMARY.

(Erase heading not required.)

SECRET.

35th DIVISIONAL AMMUNITION COLUMN.

From 1st APRIL 1918
To. 30th APRIL 1918

VOLUME 27.

Vol 27

B Bowman.
Lt. Col. R.H.A.
Comdg. 35. D.A.C. R.A.

Army Form C. 2118.

WAR DIARY
INTELLIGENCE SUMMARY.
(Erase heading not required.)

APRIL 1918

Place	Date	Hour	Summary of Events and Information	Remarks and references to Appendices
Sheet 62 D.2 B.30 x C.3	1st		At FRECHENCOURT. Billeting parties sent to PONT NOYELLES. 3728 Rounds gun ammunition to Battery wagon lines	MA
Sheet 62 D.2 H.18 a.	2nd		Fine day. Left FRECHENCOURT 10 A.M., arrived PONT NOYELLES 11 A.M. 1392 Rounds gun ammunition to Battery wagon lines	Rest
ditto	3rd		Weather fine. Lecture by C.O. to officers 6 P.M. 1828 Rounds gun ammunition to Battery W. Lines	Rest
ditto	4th		Very wet day. R. Echelon received orders to be ready to move at ½ hours notice. C.R.A. visited Column. 6.8 Remounts reported to Column [66 mules. 2 horses]. Very poor lot. 2,302 Rounds to Battery W.L. 6168 Rounds to Battery W. Lines	MA
ditto	5th		Wet weather.	MA
ditto	6th		Bad weather. 10 Gunners posted to 152 Bde. 2096 Rounds to Battery W.L. 2 " " 153 "	MA
ditto	7th		Rain & Hail showers. 1360 Rounds to Battery W. Lines	MA
ditto	8th		Wet weather. B. Echelon moved to TOUTEN COURT. 1612 Rounds to Battery W. Lines	MA
ditto	9th		Dull day. Received warning order to hand over to 3rd & 6th AUSTRALIAN A.F.A. Bdes & to proceed to move train area on 13th in. C.O. visited B. Echelon at TOUTENCOURT. 2668 Rounds to Battery W.L.	MA

PONT NOYELLES

Army Form C. 2118.

WAR DIARY
or
INTELLIGENCE SUMMARY.

(Erase heading not required.)

APRIL 1918

Place	Date	Hour	Summary of Events and Information	Remarks and references to Appendices
Sheet 6 + D H18a. PONT NOYELLES	10th		Received order at 3.15 A.M. to send 10 Mounted men to act as dispatch riders to 35th Div. Signal Order Cancelled later, as negro Guild only to be mounted on mules. Confirmation of order to move on 13th inst. received. Lt HEANEY posted to No.1 Section from No.3 Section. 1 Corporal posted to 157 Bde. 10 x 4 rounds to Battery Wagon Lines instead of 13th.	M.H.
ditto	11th		Fine weather. Orders received to move on 12th inst. Lt. CHAMBERS detailed as member of F.G.C.M. of 159 Bde. Major Lt. MMP Burns handed over to 3 + 6 AUSTRALIAN A.F.A. Brigade Relief completed by 11 A.M.	M.H.
ditto + Sheet 57 D V.2.a.b.c.	12th		Fine weather. Left PONT NOYELLES 10.45 A.M. arrived TOUTENCOURT 1.15 P.M. via BEHENCOURT CONTAY Hqrs on CONTAY road just at entrance to village. No. 1 + 2 Sections on HARPONVILLE road 500 yards from village. CPA. visited Hqrs. in afternoon. C.O. + Adjutant visited dump of (amm). Lt. H. BOWDITCH posted to Column, but to remain on Corps Reserve ammunition dump.	M.H.
ditto	13th		Fine weather. Lt CHAMBERS Posted to No.2 Section from No.1 Section. Lt HOLDER " " No.3 " " " No.2 " 2/Lt BLAIR " " No.1 " " " No.3 " 2/Lt PLAYLE " " No.3 " " " No.2 "	M.H.
ditto TOUTENCOURT	14th		Corps Commander visited Hqrs. Wet + Stormy weather. Working party for 77th A.F.A. Bde. Hqrs. G.O.C. Division visited Hqrs.	M.H. Return 77 AFA

Army Form C. 2118.

WAR DIARY
INTELLIGENCE SUMMARY.
(Erase heading not required.)

APRIL 1918

Place	Date	Hour	Summary of Events and Information	Remarks and references to Appendices
Sheet 57D V2 a.k.c.	15th		Fine hot cold weather. Capt SMITH evacuated to hospital sick.	
ditto.	16th		Wet morning fine afternoon. D.A.C. defence scheme organised. 2 Officers & 50 O.R. per Section, 1 officer & 60 O.R. from HQrs arrived with 3 Lewis Guns & 150 Rifles.	
ditto	17th		Weather fine in morning & wet later. D.D.V.S. 3rd Army inspected animals of Column. Lt. DE TANASZ Lanarkshire Yeomanry to B2 Section.	
ditto	18th		Wet weather	
ditto	19th		Snow. G.O.C. Div. visited B. Echelons & Ervillecourt hrs. Self satisfied with everything. Lt HEANEY attached ACHEUX mulehead ammunition dump.	
ditto	20th		Capt WILKINSON returned Lt. HEANEY at ACHEUX dump. Lt HEANEY to 2/R BLACK start new dump for 35th D.A. near HARPONVILLE.	
ditto	21st		Fine weather. C.O. & adjutant ins'd dumps.	
ditto	22nd		Fine weather. 1500 rounds to Battery Positions.	

WAR DIARY
INTELLIGENCE SUMMARY
(Erase heading not required.)

Army Form C. 2118.

APRIL 1918.

Place	Date	Hour	Summary of Events and Information	Remarks and references to Appendices
	23rd		Fine weather. 5 wagons sent drawing supplies from 159 Bde. Battle positions. C.R.A. visited B Echelon & expressed satisfaction	
	24th		Dull day. Above wagons carried on. { 1 gunner & 1 driver posted to 157 Bde. 3 gunners posted to 159 - 5 in hospital	
	25th		Fine weather. Capt SMITH returned from 157 Bde. 900 rounds to 157 Bde	
	26th		Fine weather. 4 wagons drawing supplies from 79th Bde. Positions	
	27th		Unsettled weather. Above fatigues continued	
	28th		Dull day. 7 O.R. posted to A.D.T.M.O. as reinforcements	
	29th		C.O. selected teams of mules & go to batteries in place. 7 horses to be sent to Column. 8 gunners posted from 4 gunners arrived posted to 157 Bde. - 159 Bde " 4 " x 5 " " - 159 Bde.	
	30th		Very wet day. Lt. DE TAN ASZ attached to 159 Bde. Orders received to draw ammunition from CONTAY dump, & deliver to Battery wagon lines till dump is cleared.	

SHEET 57A
7.2 a.f.c. 0 + 8
10 / 8 TEN COIT

Army Form C. 2118.

WAR DIARY
— or —
INTELLIGENCE SUMMARY.
(Erase heading not required.)

Vol 28

Secret.

35th DIVISIONAL AMMUNITION COLUMN

From 1st MAY 1918
To 31st MAY 1918

Volume 28.

[signature]
Capt. R.F.A.
Comdg. 35th Divl. Amm. Column.

WAR DIARY
INTELLIGENCE SUMMARY
(Erase heading not required.)

Army Form C. 2118.

MAY 1918.

Place	Date	Hour	Summary of Events and Information	Remarks and references to Appendices
TOUTENCOURT	1st		BG, RA, 5th Corps visited Column & expressed satisfaction at condition of animals & drivers as reinforcements from 12th Div. Ammunition issued 1084 rounds	1/4
	2nd		Fine day. Ammunition dumps at HARPONVILLE handed over to 17th Div. Dumps at CONTAY taken over from 63rd Div. also reserve dump at U16 c. Amn issued 3032 rounds.	1/4
	3rd		Weather fine. 11 Mules remounts received. 1798 rounds amn issued	1/4
	4th		Three 18 pounder anti tank guns drawn from CANDAS to BEAU... hauled to base. 1960 rounds amn issued	1/4
	5th		Church Parade. Lt HEANEY & L.C.R proceeded to ROUEN for remount duty. Weather showery. 1756 rounds amn issued	1/4
	6th		Fine day. Dragoons RE Fittings. 736 rounds amn issued	1/4
	7th		Very wet morning, cleared later. 1932 rounds amn issued	1/4
	8th		Weather fine. Lieut. Col. DORMAN proceeded on 30 days leave to U.K. Capt BARNETT assumed command of Column. 4054 rounds amn & gunner reinforcements to the base.	1/4
	9th		Fine weather. 987 rounds amn issued	1/4

WAR DIARY

Army Form C. 2118

MAY 1918

INTELLIGENCE SUMMARY

(Erase heading not required.)

Place	Date	Hour	Summary of Events and Information	Remarks and references to Appendices
TOUTENCOURT	10th		Weather fine. Transport & horses to 90 clerks for transliny Co. for taking up material up the line. 6906 rounds amn issued	
	11th		Dull day. Hqrs. shelled with H.V. gun, no damage or casualties. 4 G.S. wagons detailed to clear (X) battery position of supplies. Lt G WEBSTER detailed as member of F.G.C.M. 1848 rounds amn. issued	
	12th		Weather dull. 604 rounds amn issued	
	13th		Wet weather. Working party of 6 men to 159 Bde. Salvage. Commenced under Lt. TREWMAN. 592 rounds amn. issued	
	14th		Weather fine. "Ammunition supply for moving battle" test. DAC. Hqrs opened in V.16.a from 8 am. 1478 to 8 pm 1578, taking everything into consideration the scheme was a success. 1826 rounds amn. issued	
	15th		C.P.A. inspected Horses & Harness of B. Echelon & Spares keys. Sets fed with Oates. 10 Drivers Rein-forcements from 1st Div. 1044 rounds amn. issued	
	16th		Weather fine. Reserve dumps cleared. 1894 rounds amn. issued	

WAR DIARY
INTELLIGENCE SUMMARY.
(Erase heading not required.)

Army Form C. 2118.

MAY 1918

Place	Date	Hour	Summary of Events and Information	Remarks and references to Appendices
TOUTENCOURT	17th		Weather fine. Salvage & R.E. work continued. 1564 rounds issued	
	18th		Very heavy bombardment in afternoon. 4 drivers mustered as Gunners. 2270 rounds amm. issued	
	19th		Fine day. C.O. visited dumps. Lieut. H. BOWDITCH awarded Military Cross. 1490 rounds amm issued. Lecture to Assistants & Orderly Officers by Major HOLLAND, attended by H. HARDY. 3444 rounds amm issued	
	20th		Weather fine	
	21st		C.R.A. visited Hqrs. Weather fine. 1346 rounds amm issued	
	22nd		Capt. T.F.M. WILKINSON struck off strength of 35th Div Arty & on taking over duties of Sub Area Commandant BEAUVESNE. 1194 rounds amm issued	
	23rd		Divl Salvage Officer 8640 rounds amm issued began detailed search in Sub Salvage.	
	24th		Lieut. Col. D.E. FORMAN. Capt. L.W. BARNETT & B.S.M. KEYS mentioned in despatches. 2672 Rounds amm issued	
	25th		Weather fine. 1406 Rounds amm issued	

WAR DIARY
or
INTELLIGENCE SUMMARY
(Erase heading not required.)

Army Form C. 2118.

MAY 1918

Place	Date	Hour	Summary of Events and Information	Remarks and references to Appendices
	26th		Inspection by G.O.C. Division, who expressed himself pleased with the turn out of the Guard. 948 rounds S.A.A.	
	27th		Co. visited dump. 2642 rounds issued. Weather fine.	
	28th		F.G.C.M. No 14 5587 Driver H.T. PHILLIPS charged with desertion found guilty — sentenced to 3 years P.S. Lt. R. HUNTER posted to 151st Bde. RFA 5974 rounds issued. Fine weather.	
	29th		6,170 rounds amn. issued.	
	30th		4 men posted to D.T.M.O. Adjutant visited dump. 2326 rounds issued. 1328 rounds amn. issued	
	31st		Fine weather	

Rest of May. At ST. LOUITENCOURT.

Army Form C. 2118.

WAR DIARY
INTELLIGENCE SUMMARY.
(Erase heading not required.)

Instructions regarding War Diaries and Intelligence Summaries are contained in F. S. Regs., Part II. and the Staff Manual respectively. Title pages will be prepared in manuscript.

Vol 29

SECRET

35th DIVISIONAL AMMUNITION COLUMN.

— o — FROM 1st JUNE 1918 — o —

—— To 30th JUNE 1918. ——

—◇— VOLUME 29 —◇—

P. Churchill Major R.F.A.
Cmdg. 35th Div. Amm. Column

Place	Date	Hour	Summary of Events and Information	Remarks and references to Appendices

WAR DIARY / INTELLIGENCE SUMMARY

Army Form C. 2118.

JUNE 1918

Place: TOUTEN COURT SHEET 57D B2a

Date	Hour	Summary of Events and Information	Remarks
1st		Weather fine. All O.R's trains out with ammunition to hand direct to battery positions. 8556 rounds ammn. issued. Lt SMITH proceeded to HALBY-LES-PERNOIS. Lt to proceed to	
2nd		Church parade. Lt SMITH returned with remount ft Angeles. 770 rounds ammn issued	
3rd		CRA inspected remounts. Batteries drew pans at 4 P.S. 1548 rounds ammn issued	
4th		Fine weather. Mobile Ammunition Supply Scheme. New A.R.P. selected in T.5 [Sheet 57D] in the from R.M.9 4 = 45 R.M.9 5 - Every tng went along (probably 9 x rounds ammn issued 2/Lt RAXIE posted to T.M. Battery from 103 f.c.	
5th		Fine weather France	
6th		F.G.C.M. 10 am. Gr Mc DONALD informed sit 13th Bn 1772 rounds ammn issued	
7th		Lt Col FORMAN proceed on leave to U.K. [Present 8th Division] under to take over command of 33rd Bde	
8th		Fine weather *[Rate into reserve in 8th] 4788 rounds ammn issued	

WAR DIARY

INTELLIGENCE SUMMARY

Army Form C. 2118.

JUNE 1918

Place	Date	Hour	Summary of Events and Information	Remarks and references to Appendices
TO OVEZ EN COURT	9th		Church Parade. Lt. Col. FORMAN proceeded to join 8th Div. Arty. Capt. BARNETT assumed Command of Column. 3112 rounds amm. issued.	
	10th		Weather wet. 2988 rounds amm. issued.	
	11th		Fine day. 3 reinforcements from Base w. 5 rounds issued	
	12th		Fine weather. CRA. inspected staffs. 3 O.P. kept. Reinforcements 1428 rounds amm issued	
	13th		From 38th Div. Miss G. PURCELL from 17th DAC. appointed to 35th DAC. B. Echelon. Shell took H.V. shot to Armand. 632 rounds issued.	
SHEET 57d A	14th		No damage. Fine day. Gunnery in morning. CO. & 4th yet in-lay [illegible] warning order for relief by 1/2 DAC recieved. 500 rounds amm. Received orders to move to RAINCHEVAL area & that there canceled till 17th	
	15th		Fine weather. H.Q. moved to BON OREILLES O.25.c.7.2 (Sht. 57D) 1512 rounds issued	
025.C.9.7. Sheet 57D	16th		A Echelon moved to camp in N.30.b.L.7.57. B. Echelon & remainder received the following	
	17th		From E. VILLERS N.21.d.7.6 (Sht. 57D) Batteries received the following	

WAR DIARY
INTELLIGENCE SUMMARY.
(Erase heading not required.)

Army Form C. 2118.

JUNE 1918

Place: Bois d'Offretel Sh 51b O.15.d.7.6.

Date	Hour	Summary of Events and Information	Remarks and references to Appendices
18th		Fine weather. C.O. + Adjt. visited B. Sheldon	
19th		Showery weather. Orders received that all P.F. in gun teams to be reduced to 4 animals.	
20th		Weather showery. PGCM. Drivers Knight & No 2 Section left stops to the Brew.	
21st		Fine weather. No 1 Section held shots for the men. DADVS inspected animals	
22nd		Left for DIEPPE. Training Programme previous to leaving here continued	
23rd		Fine weather. Training Programme continued	
24th		Church parade. lt Campbell left for DIEPPE. Lt. Saw thro Articles. H.Q. held shots for the men	
25th		Showery day. C.R.A. visited H.Q. Training continued	
26th		Fine weather. Training Programme continued	
		Weather fine. Training contd.	

Army Form C. 2118.

WAR DIARY
INTELLIGENCE SUMMARY.
(Erase heading not required.)

JUNE 1918.

Place	Date	Hour	Summary of Events and Information	Remarks and references to Appendices
Bois Grefiel 045d 7.6 Sheet 57c	27th		2/Lt SMITH had an accident & was removed slightly off & 21 in court. A draw charge for O.O. C.O. and 2nd Section Commanders judged turn out for M/Gen. FRANKS CMG it rained. L.O.R wounded by machine gun shot from hostile aircraft.	
	28th		Field day. Maj-Gen RUNCELL Inspector of F.G.C.M. Conference attended by all available officers at M.VI. Practice alarm given. Stand to tubes take 5 hours.	
	29th		Sgt Kirby Trumpeter Off to home. The weather continues recent & Retrain all Dominions CANDAS night of 1st & 2nd July.	
	30th		CRA visited H.Q. Fine weather	

Army Form C. 2118.

WAR DIARY
or
INTELLIGENCE SUMMARY.
(Erase heading not required.)

SECRET

Vol 30

35th DIVISIONAL AMMUNITION COLUMN.

From 1st July 1918
To 31st July 1918

VOLUME 30

L. Grenvell, Major R.F.A.
Cmdg. 35th Div. Amm. Column.

Army Form C. 2118.

WAR DIARY
or
INTELLIGENCE SUMMARY.

(Erase heading not required.)

JULY 1918

Place	Date	Hour	Summary of Events and Information	Remarks and references to Appendices
BOIS CROETTEL O.25.d.7.6 SHEET 57.D.	1st		Fine Weather { No.1 Sec. Marched out for DOULLENS 10.30 A.M. No.2 " " " CANDAS 4.00 P.M. No.3 " " " DOULLENS 8.00 PM H.Q " " " CANDAS 8.00 PM	
SHEET 27. OUDEZEELE I.18.4.1.6	2nd		No.1 Sec entrained DOULLENS 4 P.M. No.2 Sec entrained CANDAS 2.10 AM, detrained WIZERNES 2.30 PM No.3 Sec " DOULLENS 4.00 PM " ARQUES 2 PM H.Q. " CANDAS 3.45 PM " WIZERNES 7.45 PM No.1 Sec. detrained ARQUES 1.30 AM & Marched to OUDEZEELE.	
ditto	3rd		HQ No.2 Sec & No.3 Sec arrived & camped in remnts of OUDEZEELE Shortly after Midnight. Weather fine & Shelon hutmt & rounds STEENVOORDE Sheet 27 Q.2.d.7.2	
ditto ditto STEENVOORDE Q.I.C.2.5	4th		Column Marched out to STEENVOORDE-TEDEGHEM area No.1 Sec. P11.C.9.9 No.2 Sec P12.d.4.7 HQ Q.I.C.2.5 Weather Fine	
ditto	5th		A.R.P. formed R.I.d.2.5 SHEET 27 Weather Good Ammunition delivered to battery positions. 7368 rounds issued Capt. Boydton B.G.R.A. Corps visited Column Lt. Boydton posted to 63rd D.A. with effect from 27.6.18 Weather bus settled 6452 rounds amn. issued	
ditto	6th		Weather wet. 3548 rounds amn issued	
ditto	7th			
ditto	8th		Weather fine 9/10 misted dump 992 rounds issued	

WAR DIARY
or
INTELLIGENCE SUMMARY.

(Erase heading not required.)

Army Form C. 2118.

JULY 1918

Place: **JANSCAT FME** R.I.C. T.S. SHEET 27

Date	Hour	Summary of Events and Information	Remarks and references to Appendices
9th		Weather wet. 2991 rounds amm issued	
10th		Showery day. 2114 rounds amm issued	
11th		ditto. 1646 rounds amm issued	
12th		Capt. BARNETT & JENKINS proceeded on 10 days leave in France. CRA noted 2/Lt LINDLEY attached & taken on instruction. Showery. 1941 rounds amm issued.	
13th		Fine weather. Lts. WEBSTER & SMITH, J.S.) proceeded to ROUEN for Indian Courses of Instruction. 1356 rounds amm. 11 O.R. reinforcements from base. 60 +M.M.S. dismounted Section. 3044 rounds amm issued	
14th		Showery day. Church parade.	
15th		Fine day. 2/Lt CAMPBELL proceeded to P.7a 7.5. Sheet 27 with 28 vehicles & formed an advanced Section 1468 rounds amm. issued	
16th		Fine weather. 3730 rounds amm. issued	

WAR DIARY
or
INTELLIGENCE SUMMARY.
(Erase heading not required.)

Army Form C. 2118.

JULY 1918

Place	Date	Hour	Summary of Events and Information	Remarks and references to Appendices
SHEET 27 PANSGATES FME R.I.G.A.T.S.	17th		Fine weather. Gnp't of Inform. int afrenm of Driver JARVIS W.S. Sea A/Adjt visited dump & forward section.	
	18th		2/Lt LINDLEY relieved at dump by officers from 38 Army Bde. & attached to forward Sec. 6688 rounds amm issued.	
	19th		Fine weather. All vehicles in A Echelon Shelter Positions 9194 rounds amm. issued.	
	20th		Fine weather. CO visited forward section & dump. RSM GILLARD returned from leave in UK. CPA noted HQ & Sections 1 + 2. 1730 rounds amm. issued	
	21st		Showery day. 2/Lt BUXTON (night posted to DAC from face) & SPALDING posted from force 2 + 35 TMB. 60 In Sheds of Sections. 2/Lt BLAIR bracketed to hospital. 2/Lt HEANEY took over dump. 5064 rounds amm. 15 strangs.	
	22nd		Fine day. Church parade. 1816 rounds issued	
	23rd		Fine weather. 5130 rounds amm issued	
			Wet day. 5 reinforcements posted to D.T.M.O 48 cartridge clips for Webleys pouches frames (495 weapons 2120 rounds issued)	

WAR DIARY
or
INTELLIGENCE SUMMARY

Army Form C. 2118

JULY 1918

Place	Date	Hour	Summary of Events and Information	Remarks and references to Appendices
SHEET 27 PANISIERES A.1. FIVE c 6.5	24th		Fine day. CO visited Majors Lee & dump. Capt. BARNETT & JENKINS returned from leave in France. 4094 rounds issued.	
	25th		Fine weather. 4. O.P. reinforcement. Hun Cartiny Coy. 2740 rounds issued. 3 wagons.	
	26th		Showery day. Hun Cartiny Coy. 3 wagons. 7308 rounds issued.	
	27th		Wet weather. B.C. & Adjt. proceeded advance Hd. dump. 9000 rounds issued. 3 wagons. per battery firing visiting till further orders.	
	28th		Fine day. Capt BARNETT to D.A. acting Staff Offr. 8946 rounds amm. issued. Capt. JENKINS to advanced section.	
	29th		Fine weather. 8690 rounds amm. issued.	
	30th		Fine weather. 6474 rounds amm. issued.	
	31st		Fine weather. C.O. visited Advanced Sec. & dump. 1 man & 7 animals wounded at D.157 batter. position. 6843 rounds amm. issued.	

Signature

Army Form C. 2118.

WAR DIARY
or
~~INTELLIGENCE SUMMARY.~~
(Erase heading not required.)

35th DIVISIONAL AMMUNITION COLUMN

From 1st AUGUST 1918
To 31st AUGUST 1918

VOLUME 31.

A. Fitzgerald Major RFA.
C mdg. 35th Dn Ammn Column.

Army Form C. 2118.

WAR DIARY
or
INTELLIGENCE SUMMARY.
(Erase heading not required.)

AUGUST 1918

Hour, Date, Place	Summary of Events and Information	Remarks and references to Appendices
1st	Weather fine.	
2nd	Showery day. Capt Foster relieved Capt Jenkins at advanced Section. Lt R.B.R returned from top. 1830 rounds ammunition issued.	
3rd	Batt FOSTEN returned L Section. Personnel Section reduced by 9 weapons. 578 rounds amn issued.	
4th	Special Church Parade & March past L Engles L 30 OR mounted 357 D.A 60 rounds. Dump advanced to hour 1170 rounds issued. Dull weather	
5th	Wet day. 726 rounds amn issued.	
6th	Fine day. RDRS I CHC inspected guns at Charm. T Epercury takes station at Couture.	
7th	Rain. Major G Vincent handed P.P.C.M. Warning order, J relief by 30 div. about 10/11. 11/15 Inspect. Received 580 rounds ammunt.	

Shed 21
Air G 715
Ramsgat FME

Army Form C. 2118.

WAR DIARY
or
INTELLIGENCE SUMMARY.
(Erase heading not required.)

AUGUST 1918

Hour, Date, Place	Summary of Events and Information	Remarks and references to Appendices
8th	Fine weather. 4 [OR] killed & 2 [OR] wounded. Stores & D.T.M.O. with G.S. wagons & trains. I.O.M. inspected all vehicles of Column & spread himself. Satisfied with condition of same. Further relief of [?] Sub div [?] 12/13 August 1918	
9th	530 rounds [?] Ammunition ready.	
10th	Fine weather. 60 rounds Ammunition.	
11th	300 rounds Ammunition issued. Fine day. 3 [?] rounds Ammn issued.	
12th	Fine day. Special church parade for King George [?] at the Minister [?]. Capt Marriott returned from D.A. Party Harvest Section returned from Reserve. Section LOCRAINE handed over to 30 D.A.C. RAMSGATE PH.P. [?] taken over from 30 D.A.C. MONTAGUE " " 10 G.S. wagons on loan to Divnl Transport for conveying of [?]	
13	Weather fine. No [?] men dispatched in [?] on [?]	

Sheet 27
R.F.C. & 5
RAMSGATE P.M.C.

Army Form C. 2118.

WAR DIARY
or
INTELLIGENCE SUMMARY

(Erase heading not required.)

AUGUST 1918

Place	Date	Hour	Summary of Events and Information	Remarks and references to Appendices
	14th		Fine weather. Lt. HARDY proceeded on leave in France. Parties to training programme. Worked fine. Harvesting cont'd.	
	15th		Training programme. Worked fine. Harvesting cont'd, starting progressing.	
	16th		Fine day. Training & Harvesting Cont'd.	
	17th		Lt HEANEY proceeded on leave U.K. Training cont'd.	
	18th		Fine weather. 10 O.R. began to harvesting. Company went to Church.	
	19th		10. O.S. began & harvesting Cont'd.	
	20th		Very warm weather. Training & Harvesting Cont'd. Who began & harvesting. Anita. Guns received from Base for training.	
	21st		Very warm. Lt JOHNSON proceeded on leave U.K. Training cont'd.	
	22nd		Weather fine. Training. 24 began arm'd instruction to stalls & rifles. Commenced F. McAfee Lat W.D.	

Lieut. ?
R.I.C. 2.I.C.
PRI Sergt Fine.

WAR DIARY
or
INTELLIGENCE SUMMARY.
(Erase heading not required.)

Army Form C. 2118.

AUGUST 1918

Place	Date	Hour	Summary of Events and Information	Remarks and references to Appendices
	23rd		Fine weather. B. inspn. Horse 11.03 to. Lad Apping football Competition	
	24th		Left Morning Service. Afternoon B.A.C. sports. C.R.A. & staff present.	
	25th		Unsettled afternoon. Church Parade	
	26th		Wet day. Rainy	
	27th		All day. Lt HARDY returned from leave in FRANCE. Date of emb...	
	28th		Showery day. Lieut JENKINS proceeded to leave to UK. Leave exp...	
	29th		Fine day. D.A. rifle competition won by No.1 Sec. D.A.C.	
	30th		Fine day. 60 rocky. Instructed that we move at once...	
			Received in afternoon to be ready to move at once. Instructions...	
			later. Finally if for this completion WB & Sec M. Div. Guns R.E.S.	
	31st		Fine weather X Corps head Qrs. Orders received...	
			except A (Rest 27). E17 L.9.7. & lay 17.36 Div Guns R.5	

Army Form C. 2118

WAR DIARY
or
INTELLIGENCE SUMMARY
(Erase heading not required.)

Vol 32

35th DIVISIONAL AMMUNITION COLUMN.

From :- 1st September 1918.
To :- 30th September 1918.

VOLUME 32.

L. Gruwell Major R.F.A.
Commanding 35th Div. Amm. Col., A.I.F.

Army Form C. 2118

WAR DIARY / INTELLIGENCE SUMMARY

(Erase heading not required.)

SEPTEMBER 1918

Place	Date	Hour	Summary of Events and Information	Remarks and references to Appendices
Sheet 27 Q.b. 2.5 PANSYGAT FARM	1st		Fine Weather. Moved from PANYS at FARM 9.30 am. Arrived PONTYPOOL CAMP. Sheet 27. E7 & 97. 12 Noon. Orders received to relieve 34th D.A. on 2nd Sept. 2/Lt HARRINGTON proceeded to CALAIS for remounts for D.A. Dump at SPENTE	M/A
Sheet 27 E7 & 97 PONTYPOOL CAMP	2nd		Fine day. Marched from PONTYPOOL CAMP 10.30 am. Arrived HAMMOEK standings Sheet 28 A25 & 1.9. 2/Lt CAMPBELL proceeded on leave to U.K. Dump taken over at LOUIS CHATEAU	M/A
HAMMOEK A25 b1.9 Sheet 28	3rd		Fine Weather. C.R.A. visited H.Q. & Sections 1 & 2. 2/Lt HEARNEY returned from leave in U.K. 67 rounds issued.	M/A
ditto	4th		New dump started. ORILLIA Sheet 28 H.2a 1.1. 2/Lt HARRINGTON arrived back from CALAIS with remounts. 2/Lt CESSFORD joined from Base. 7920 rounds amm. issued	M/A
ditto	5th		Fine Weather. Distribution of remounts to Brigades & D.A.C. C.R.A. present. Co. & Adjt visited dumps. 8665 rounds amm. issued	M/A
ditto	6th		Fine day. WEST SPUR dump G4 b.4.6. taken over from 66th Div Arty. ORILLIA landed over to 147th Div Arty. 1700 rounds issued. MORRIS + WISE dumps taken over from 66th D.A.	M/A
ditto	7th		Wet day. D.A.C. Horses to Camp in EIKHOEK area. H.Q. F28 & 7.2 Sheet 27. CHATEAU dump handed over to 147th D.A.	M/A
EIKHOEK F28 & 7.2 Sheet 27	8th		Wet weather. 900 rounds issued.	M/A
ditto	9th		Showery day. 2880 rounds amm. issued	M/A

[signature]

WAR DIARY
or
INTELLIGENCE SUMMARY

(Erase heading not required.)

Army Form C. 2118

SEPTEMBER 1918

Place	Date	Hour	Summary of Events and Information	Remarks and references to Appendices
EIKHOEK Sheet 27 F28.b.7.	10th		Wet weather. B. Echelon moved from STEENMOORDE to BOOME CAMP L.2,13,b,13. Capts. BARNETT & REPEN proceeded on leave to U.K. 824 rounds issued	M.H.
ditto	11th		Wet day. Final of Div. Arty. Football Competition. D.157.V. No.2 Bde D.A.C. Div. 157 gave No 2 Bde nil. C.R.A. presented medals to winners & runners up.	M.H.
ditto	12th		Dir. General present for a short time. 1130 rounds ammn issued. 18 G.S. wagons sent to home standings & material for home standings & staples. 608 rounds ammn. issued.	M.H.
ditto	13th		Fine day. D.A. gunnery School opened at No 2 Sec. under R.S.M. GILLARD instructed same in animal management. Capt J JENKINS returned from leave in U.K.	M.H.
ditto	14th		Showery day. Orders received to move to new area S.W. of PERINGHE. INDIAN PERSONNEL arrived from ROUEN under Lt. T.S. SMITH.	M.H.
ditto	15th		Fine day. D.A.C. moved to new camp H.Q. Z.18.d.9.7. Ration 27. A.Echelon to Z.15.b.9.2 & 9.5. Ration 27. 76 rounds ammn issued	M.H.
ENTYNLAND Sheet 27/6 L.18.d.9.7. Sheet 27 (Porter Camp)	16th		Fine weather. H.Q. moved to L.18.a.8.7. C.R.A. visited H.Q. & Sections 1,2,3. B.Echelon received orders to move to N&B 12 Camp L.10.C.8.2. M.H. HARRINGTON posted to 157 Brigade 800 rounds ammn issued on 17th Sept	M.H.
L.18.a.8.7 Sheet 27	17th		Fine day. B.Echelon arrived in NUBIC CAMP L.10.C.8.2. 2550 rounds ammn issued	M.H.

M Kenzie Major

Army Form C. 2118

WAR DIARY
or
INTELLIGENCE SUMMARY
(Erase heading not required.)

SEPTEMBER 1918

III

Place	Date	Hour	Summary of Events and Information	Remarks and references to Appendices
Moose Jaw L.18a 8:7	18th		Fine weather. New dump formed at VANCOUVER H14 & S.8. 10 64 rounds amm. issued. 24 men attached to Battery on advanced position.	MM
ditto	19th		Fine day. Advanced D.A.C. H.Q. formed H.8.A.36. Sheet 28. BISHOPSGATE CAMP No. 17. Advanced Section under Capt. JENKINS formed at G.9 & 5.8. Sheet 28. 70 N. FORM. 6330 rounds issued.	BMM
ditto	20th		Fine weather. 5128 rounds amm. issued. Advanced Section assisted in getting up amm. to new position.	MM
ditto	21st		Showery weather. Advanced Section all vehicles to front position. 2 drivers wounded, 3 mules killed. 3578 rounds issued. (Lt. T.S. SMITH proceeded on leave to U.K.)	MM
ditto	22nd		Showery day. 5114 rounds amm. issued. CORDOVA dump ??? included. Battery No. ??? position included	MM
ditto	23rd		Rain in morning. Fine later. 6739 rounds amm.	MM
ditto	24th		Fine weather. 4954 rounds issued.	MM
ditto	25th		Wet day. Lt. JOHNSON relived BINGLIS at Pumps Store. Lt. KEARNEY took over dump form 2/Lt. BLAIR. 1516 rounds issued.	BMM
ditto	26th		Fine weather. 408 rounds amm. issued.	MM
Sheet 28 Moose Jaw Form H.8.C.6.2	27th		Fine day. All D.A.C. H.Q. moved to MOOSE JAW Form H.8.C.6.2. BINGLIS & 2/Lt. BLAIR proceeded on leave to U.K. 1106 rounds amm. issued.	BMM

Army Form C. 2118

WAR DIARY
—or—
INTELLIGENCE SUMMARY
(Erase heading not required.)

IV   SEPTEMBER 1918

Place	Date	Hour	Summary of Events and Information	Remarks and references to Appendices
MOOSE JAW FARM Sheet 57 H.6.C.6.x.	28		Wet day. All Sections Moved forward to HALIFAX & VANCOUVER CAMP. Sheet 27 H.14.a & b. A.R.R. moved forward to HOWE CAMP. H.24.b. 6 & 8 rounds Amm. issued.	M.H.
ditto	29th		Fine. Rain in evening. Weather hot & Steamy. Orders to be ready to move received in Cancelled in evening.	M.H.
	30th		Move on morning of 30th instant. Rec. G.S. wagons out cleaning & oiling and Battery positions & taking amm. forward to TRANSPORT PARK I²a S²² Ref. 28. B. & later moved forward & PLANE POST FARM I.7.65.4 Rest 28. Very wet & stormy day. D.A.C. A solemn app moved at 17.30 am to I.7.21.d. A.R.P. Formed at TRANSPORT FARM I¹a S¹ Rec. returns & TRANSPORT FARM.	M.H.

M.H.

Army Form C. 2118.

WAR DIARY
of
INTELLIGENCE SUMMARY.
(Erase heading not required.)

WC 33

SECRET

35th DIVISIONAL AMMUNITION COLUMN. R.F.A.

FROM :- 1st OCTOBER 1918
TO :- 31st OCTOBER 1918

VOLUME. 33

E. Criswell Maj. R.F.A.
Comdg. 35th D.v. Ammn Column

Army Form C. 2118.

WAR DIARY
INTELLIGENCE SUMMARY.
(Erase heading not required.)

OCTOBER 1918

Place	Date	Hour	Summary of Events and Information	Remarks and references to Appendices
SHEET 28 I.2.C. S.J. TRANSPORT FARM	1st		100 animals for Section lacking ammunition to ordnance dumps at ZANVOORDE Sheet 28. P.3.C.S.B. Salvaging of Feu lootins continued. Fine day. 2024 rounds issued. 2300 rounds salved. 4 of Indian Personnel wounded.	PM
	2nd		Fine weather. 200 rounds issued 266 rounds salved	PM Ritis
	3rd		Fine day. Salvaging of German guns commenced (724)	PM
	4th		Wet day. 4 German Guns Salved, also Several T.M's & Machine Guns. 868 rounds issued 900 rounds Salved. Lt Campbell proceeded to CALAIS with 50 O.R. (Indians) for remounts	PM
	5th		Showery day. Salvaging continued	Fine
	6th		Fine weather. Trams Sent to 157 & 159 to help move their weapons lines, owing to Casualties to their Animals. No 3 Section moved to GHELUVELT, but were ordered to return to BLAUWE POORT farm later in day. 2648 rounds issued 2000 rounds Salved. A.R.P formed in T.29.a. Sheet 28. CORNWALL A.R.P	PM
	7th		Fine day. Lt CAMPBELL returned from CALAIS with remounts Lt J.S. SMYTH rejoined from leave in U.K. 2498 rounds issued 4064 rounds salved, also L.T.M's.	Rly
	8th		Fine weather. Capt BARNETT rejoined from leave in U.K. 2.O.R wounded 3 mules killed & 1 horse & 1 mule wounded 2698 rounds issued. 1218 rounds Salved.	PM

Anhomy Clifts

WAR DIARY
INTELLIGENCE SUMMARY
(Erase heading not required.)

Army Form C. 2118

OCTOBER 1918

Place	Date	Hour	Summary of Events and Information	Remarks and references to Appendices
SHEET 28 TRANS BAY FARM I.2.a S.4.	9th		Fine weather. Advanced lines reconnoitred in K.1 & 2 Sheet 28. 1158 rounds issued. 4529 rounds Salvd.	19/M
	10th		Dull day. 2730 rounds issued. 6262 rounds Salvd.	19/M
	11th		Dull weather. 3880 rounds issued. 3303 rounds Salvd.	19/M
	12th		Dull weather. Lt HARDY proceeded on leave to UK. Lt INGLIS + 2/Lt SMITH rejoined from leave in UK. 3950 rounds Salvd.	19/M
	13th		Very wet day. C.O. attended Conference at STRAIN G. CASTLE. Sections 1 + 2 Q.F. Wagons attached to 157 + 159 Bdes. respectively. H.Q. moved to T.29.a.S.S. Sheet 28.	19/M
Sheet 28 T.29.a.S.S. GHELUVELT	14th		Fine day. H.Q. Shelled. 1 O.R. killed 1 horse killed & 1 wounded. Horses moved to W. of GHELUVELT. A.R.P. formed at PEUTEVIN WOOD K.22.6.5.8 Sheet 28. 4 Mules killed ~ 1 O.R. wounded. All G.S. Wagons out with ammunition. No 3 Section moved forward to GHELUVELT.	19/M
ditto.	15th		Still day. No 3 Section moved to T.30.a.5.4. Sheet 28. 1 O.R. killed 1 horse + 2 mules killed. No 2 advanced Section at I.19.5.8.0 Sheet 28. No 1 advanced Section at K.17.C.0.0. Sheet 28.	19/M

Army Form C. 2118

WAR DIARY
INTELLIGENCE SUMMARY
(Erase heading not required.)

OCTOBER 1918

Instructions regarding War Diaries and Intelligence Summaries are contained in F.S. Regs., Part II. and the Staff Manual respectively. Title Pages will be prepared in manuscript.

Place	Date	Hour	Summary of Events and Information	Remarks and references to Appendices
SHEET 28 Jga SS GHELUVELT	16th		Wet weather. HQ & G.S. wagons moved to PEUTEVIN WOOD Sheet 28 K22 b.5.8. A.R.P. formed at L.22.C.3.7 Sheet 28 moved forward from CORNWALL. New A.R.P. 10 G.S. wagons from No.3. section to assist. Issued 5669 rounds. Capt SMITH proceeded on leave to U.K.	MM
Sheet 28 K22 b.5.8. PEUTEVIN WOOD	17th		Fine day. New A.R.P. formed at DAD12EELEHOEK Sheet 28 I.14.t. 20 new (?) men from T.M.S. to assist on A.R.P. 50 remounts arrived. 2773 rounds amnn. issued.	MM
ditto	18th		Fine weather. Lt CESSFORD sick to hospital. 3300 rounds issued	MM
ditto	19th		Dull day. Sabraging commenced. 3931 rounds Sabrad. 3948 rounds issued	MM
ditto	20th		Dull day. SAC Complete moved to BISSEGHEM. G.35.a Sheet 29 A.R.P. formed at G.35.a. 3-8. Sheet 29. 1389 rounds ammn. issued 2 mules wounded	MM
Sheet 29 G35a BISSEGHEM	21st		Very wet day. 184 rounds ammn sabrad	MM
ditto	22nd		Fine day. Sections moved to E. edge of WEVELGHEM. CORNWALL A.R.P. cleared.	MM
ditto	23rd		Fine weather. Sections Sabraging ammn. from vacated battery positions. 960 rounds ammn. issued	MM

1875 Wt. W593/826 1,000,000 4/15 J.B.C. & A. A.D.S.S./Forms/C. 2118.

WAR DIARY
INTELLIGENCE SUMMARY

Army Form C. 2118.

IV / OCTOBER 1918

Place	Date	Hour	Summary of Events and Information	Remarks and references to Appendices
SHEET 29 G.35.a. BISSEGHEM.	24th		Dull day. 4 O.R. volunteered to take forward Mobile T.M. received to clear BISSEGHEM A.R.P. by 27th Oct 1554 rounds issued. 1 horse killed.	10/4
ditto.	25th		Fine weather. Mobile T.M. started. 1626 rounds ammn. issued.	13/4
ditto.	26th		Fine day. No. 3 Section moved to SWEVEGHEM. New Campos near COURTRAI reconnoitred also near SWEVEGHEM. A.R.P. formed at X roads in 0.14.d. Sheet 29. 1300 rounds issued.	14/4
ditto.	27th		Fine day. Sections 1 & 2 moved to SWEVEGHEM. + HQ to 0.9.25 Sheet 29. 1056 rounds ammn. issued.	15/4
Sheet 29 0.9.C.25.	28th		Fine day. 1 horse killed by bomb from E.A. 392 rounds ammn issued	16/4
ditto.	29th		Fine weather. Lt HARDY returned from leave on U.K. 24 O.R. weapons to 157 taking prisoners with annul. 2077 rounds issued	17/4
ditto.	30th		Fine day. 980 rounds ammn. issued. 14 animals Conf. to Div. Signals army to casualties from bombing by E.A.s	18/4
ditto.	31st		Dull day. 4678 rounds issued. Total Salvage during Month 41279 rounds ammunition. 31 German found. Several T.M.s & M.G.s	19/4

Army Form C. 2118.

WAR DIARY
or
INTELLIGENCE SUMMARY.

(Erase heading not required.)

35th DIVISIONAL AMMUNITION COLUMN

From:- 18th November 1918.
to:- 30th November 1918.

Volume:- 34

Kenneth Latham R.F.A.
2nd Lieut. 35th Div Amm. Col. A.F.

Army Form C. 2118

WAR DIARY
or
INTELLIGENCE SUMMARY
(Erase heading not required.)

NOVEMBER 1918

Place	Date	Hour	Summary of Events and Information	Remarks and references to Appendices
Sheet 29 O.9.C.2.8.	1st		Fine day. Orders received to take over Camps of 4th DAC. Courtrai on 2nd Nov. Capt. H. Smith rejoined from leave in U.K. Ammunition issued nil.	
ditto.	2nd		Fine day. Column moved to Courtrai. Took over lines & billets of 4th DAC. HQ at Huef N°35. Toekomst Strsst. Knokke ARP. Handed over to 41st DAC.	
Courtrai Sheet 29 H.32.a.68	3rd		Fine day. C.O. attended Conference at Div Arty. 10.30 hours.	
ditto	4th		Fine weather. Orders received to move to Sweveghem area on 5th Nov.	
ditto	5th		Wet day. DAC moved to Sweveghem. HQ at Sheet 29. O.3. Central.	
Sheet 29 O.3 Central	6th		Dull weather. ARP formed at Krote Sheet 29 O.4.C.8.6. Capt. Ten Kins proceeded to U.K. on month's special leave. Capt. Burnett received orders to join 14th Div. DAC as Staff Captain. 2 I.G.S. from N°3 Section with volunteer drivers from all sections attached to DTMO for conveying T.M. ammunition. 1356 rounds amm. issued.	
ditto	7th		Dull day. 6 wagons amm. to each battery 159 Bde. 3 horses & 1 team to DTMO for German H. gun & ammunition. 2548 rounds amm. issued. L/27762 Cpl. E.G. Webb Awarded Military Medal. XIX Corps orders 6.11.18	

Army Form C. 2118.

WAR DIARY
or
INTELLIGENCE SUMMARY.

(Erase heading not required.)

NOVEMBER 1918

Instructions regarding War Diaries and Intelligence Summaries are contained in F. S. Regs., Part II. and the Staff Manual respectively. Title pages will be prepared in manuscript.

Place	Date	Hour	Summary of Events and Information	Remarks and references to Appendices
Sheet 29 O.3. Central	8th		Dull day. Capt. BURNETT proceeded to 14th D.A. as Staff Capt. 3738 rounds amm. issued	
ditto	9th		Fine day. Enemy retirement reported. Orders received to move to MOLENHOEK Sheet 29 P.24, at dawn on 10th Nov. 4343 rounds ammunition issued	
ditto	10th		Fine day. Column moved at dawn to MOLENHOEK. H.Q. at P.30.a.b.5. B.R.P. formed at Sheet 29 P.24 a.53. Salvaging old battery positions commenced. 7941 rounds salved	
MOLENHOEK Sheet 29 P.30.a.6.9	11th		Wet day. Orders received that armistice to commence. Form Mops. 6 teams assisting in crossing timber for bridgeheads over the SCHELDT between TENHOVE & BERCHEM. 2713 rounds salved	
ditto	12th		Fine day. 560 rounds ammunition salved	
ditto	13th		Fine weather. Major A.C. GRINCELL proceeded on leave to U.K. Capt. H. SMYTH assumed command of Column. 1716 rounds amm. salved	
ditto	14th		Fine day. Salvaging continued 1650 rounds salved	
ditto	15th		Fine weather. 2/Lt CENFORD struck off strength & to ENGLAND. {No. 102152 Dr (A/L Bdr) W. FRANCIS awarded Military Medal. IX Corps Orders 15.11.18} 1482 rounds ammunition salved	

Army Form C. 2118.

WAR DIARY
or
INTELLIGENCE SUMMARY.
(Erase heading not required.)

NOVEMBER 1918

Instructions regarding War Diaries and Intelligence Summaries are contained in F. S. Regs., Part II. and the Staff Manual respectively. Title pages will be prepared in manuscript.

Place	Date	Hour	Summary of Events and Information	Remarks and references to Appendices
MOLENHOEK Sheet 9 P.30.a.6.9.	16th		Fine weather. Orders received to move to CUERNE area near COURTRAI on 17th Nov.	
ditto	17th		Fine, Cold weather. D.A.C. marched at 11.45 hours via INCOYGHEM, DEERLYCK & HARLEBEKE to CUERNE. H.Q. at Sheet 29 H.9.b.6.4. Sections in H.3 & arrived CUERNE 16 hours	
CUERNE 18th Sheet 29 H.9.b.6.4.	18th		Cold weather, some rain & sleet. Chair of Wheelers to Military Commandant COURTRAI for use in Civilian Sanitary Cart. General cleanup & refitting. Salvaging of ammunition in vicinity of dumps	
ditto	19th		Fine weather.	
ditto	20th		Dull foggy day. Shoe work continued	
ditto	21st		Dull weather. Lecture by Commander SPICER-SIMPSON on the doings of the fleet.	
ditto	22nd		Fine day. Meeting of Section Commanders at H.Q. & discuss Education Programme. 2/ R.M.R. officers. Lt. TRENIMAN returned from leave in U.K. Warning order to move to area west of ONSSEL about 30th Nov. received	

Army Form C. 2118

WAR DIARY
or
INTELLIGENCE SUMMARY
(Erase heading not required.)

NOVEMBER 1918

IV

Place	Date	Hour	Summary of Events and Information	Remarks and references to Appendices
CUERNE Sheet 29 H.9.6.4	23rd		Fine weather. Salvaging of S.A.A. & gun ammunition continued. 27 recruits (3 horses valuables) received from details 11th A.F.A. Bde. Lt. T. S. SMITH proceeded to GRAMMONT to fetch 8 R.F. wagons of 4th div. Materials & deliver same to 5th Army Gun park at KNOCK M.T. & Rail details. Major A.C. GRUNCELL awarded Military Cross XIV Corps orders 20.11.18 29.	RM
ditto	24th		Showery day. All horse S.A.A. & Gun ammunition handed in to BISSIGHEM & HEULE railhead dumps.	RM
ditto	25th		Fine day. 5 riders selected to go forward with army of occupation.	RM
ditto	26th		Fine weather. 6.R.A. went round all sections. Lt SMITH arrived back from GRAMMONT with 8 wagons of 4. St. Div. Mats details.	RM
ditto	27th		Fine day. 38 teams out recovering 16 guns, & 22 R.F. wagons of 4. St. D.A. details from SWEVEGHEM to St Amny Gunpark Knock. 30 wagons G.S.] attached to infantry Bdes. for move.	RM
ditto	28th		Wet day. Lt. BLAIR Sick to hospital. Final orders to march on 30 Nov to MENIN received.	RM
ditto	29th		Fine day. 11 teams out moving 11 R.F. wagons 34th D.A. details from Swevechem to Knock.	RM
ditto	30		Fine day. Column Marched to MENIN. (The College)	RM

A. Crawford Lt. RFA

Army Form C. 2118.

WAR DIARY
INTELLIGENCE SUMMARY.
(Erase heading not required.)

Vol 35

35th DIVISIONAL AMMUNITION COLUMN.

ROYAL FIELD ARTILLERY.

From 1st DECEMBER 1918.
To 31st DECEMBER 1918.

VOLUME. 35.

L. Churchill Major. MC. RFA
Cmdg. 35th DIVISIONAL AMMUNITION COLUMN.

Army Form C. 2118.

WAR DIARY
INTELLIGENCE SUMMARY
1 DECEMBER 1918

(Erase heading not required.)

Instructions regarding War Diaries and Intelligence Summaries are contained in F. S. Regs., Part II. and the Staff Manual respectively. Title pages will be prepared in manuscript.

Place	Date	Hour	Summary of Events and Information	Remarks and references to Appendices
The Cottage MENIN	1st		Column marched from MENIN 0840 hours. Arrived BROWN CAMP Sheet 28. A.22.d.9.4. at 1545 hours. Showery weather.	
BROWN CAMP Sheet 28 A.22.d.9.4	2nd		Column marched from BROWN CAMP. 08.30 hours. Arrived TERDEGHEM 12.45 hours. Fine day.	
TERDEGHEM	3rd		Column marched from TERDEGHEM at 30 hours. Arrived NIEURLET 14.30 hours. Weather wet. Major GRINNELL rejoined from leave in UK. Assumed command of Column. Lt F.R SMITH rejoined Column from air surplus. Visit through QMET	
P.10 Central			Column from air surplus. CRA motor Column.	
NIEURLET Sheet 27	4th		Fine weather.	
	5th		Fine day. No.1 Section & TMB's moved to ST MOMELIN.	
M.14.a.	6th		Dull day. 10.R.A visited Column.	
ditto	7th		Fine weather.	
ditto	8th		12 G.S. Wagons & more 2nd Army Artillery School TRIQUES. Fine day.	
ditto	9th		Fine day. Capt. JENKINS rtn from leave in UK. Major General 5 G.S. Wagons to 2nd Army Artillery School T(r?) instructed him & tillate.	
ditto	10th		Wet day. 13 rein(forcements?) arrived from base. Above wagons & Arty School.	

Army Form C. 2118.

WAR DIARY
or
INTELLIGENCE SUMMARY.
(Erase heading not required.)

Instructions regarding War Diaries and Intelligence
Summaries are contained in F. S. Regs., Part II.
and the Staff Manual respectively. Title pages
will be prepared in manuscript.

11 DECEMBER 1918

Place	Date	Hour	Summary of Events and Information	Remarks and references to Appendices
NIEURLET	11th		Dull day. 1st round Dur. Football Competition. 18 & F. V. DAC. Score 3	F DAC/12 RM
	12th		Rain at MERCKEGHEM. 4 Drivers demobilized. Presentation of Medals by G.O.C. Division at TILQUES. 80 O.R. Yeates + all officers of below present. DAC recipients: Major A.C. GRUNCELL Military Cross, 1st M. Sgt. C. DUCKWORTH M.S.M. 87767 Gr. E.G. WEBB M.M. 876106t S.G.F. WATERS M.M. Capt. JENKINS attached to 159 Bde. Bty.	RM
SHEET 27 M.14a	13th		Wet weather. Warning order received from Chrome to BAILLEUL to assist 33rd Labour Group	RM
	14th		Dull day Co. & Adjt. Reconnoitred camps for DAC in BAILLEUL area	RM
	15th		Fine weather. Camps selected for Sections of KEMMEL NEUVE EGLISE, NIEPPE. DAC Wagon M.T. Cory. footballs drawn	RM
	16th		Turn out of Competition for transport. No 3 Section winners, 5 Drivers & 2 pivotal men demobilized.	RM
	17th		Fine weather. Lt. JOHNSON conducting Demobilization. Inspn to 2nd Bty G.O.C. division Major reviewed Capt. B. No 3 Section to transport competition. Active (my) C.R.A. & all officers at TILQUES.	RM

WAR DIARY
INTELLIGENCE SUMMARY
(Erase heading not required.)

Army Form C. 2118.

III / DECEMBER 1918.

Place	Date	Hour	Summary of Events and Information	Remarks and references to Appendices
	18th		Last day to G.S. waggons to Gun Teams to deliver rations to their batteries being regained for Transport Competition. 5 miners demobilized.	
	19th		Fine weather. 14 G.S. waggons on loan to Brigades.	
	20th		Fine day.	
	21st		Fine weather. Major GRUNCELL assisted in judging of R.E. Transport Competition. 1 Private man demobilized.	
	22nd		Fine weather.	
	23rd		Wet day. CRA visited Column.	
	24th		Dull day.	
	25th		Fine weather. Usual Christmas Festivities.	
	26th		Lt. F.R.SMITH to ENGLAND. 5 te demobilized. 5 miners demobilized.	
	27th		Wet weather.	
	28th		Salvage operations commenced under an officer from this Section on duty each day last day. 1 Lorry service man demobilized.	
	29th		Salvage continued. Church parade. Wet weather.	

WAR DIARY

INTELLIGENCE SUMMARY

Army Form C. 2118.

DECEMBER 1918

Place	Date	Hour	Summary of Events and Information	Remarks and references to Appendices
NIEURLET Sheet 27 M1/a	30th		Dull weather. Orders received to send 4 3GS + 7 LGS weapons forward to S. JEAN on 2nd Jan 1919 for Salvage work.	PMcD
	31st		Fine day. C.O. + Capt SMITH reconnoitred camp for advanced section at St JEAN. Lieut HOLT joined DAC from 159 Bde. RFA. 4 miners demobilized also 1 Pivotal man + 1 Army Service man.	PMcD

P.McKay Capt

Army Form C. 2118

WAR DIARY
~~INTELLIGENCE SUMMARY~~
(Erase heading not required.)

35th Divisional Ammunition Column.
—◇— Royal Field Artillery —◇—
From 1st January 1919
To 31st January 1919.
—◇— Volume 36 —0—

Vol 36

T. Grunell, Major, R.F.A.
COMDG. 35th DIV. AM'N. COLUMN.

Instructions regarding War Diaries and Intelligence Summaries are contained in F. S. Regs., Part II. and the Staff Manual respectively. Title Pages will be prepared in manuscript.

Place	Date	Hour	Summary of Events and Information	Remarks and references to Appendices

1875 Wt. W593/826 1,000,000 4/15 J.B.C. & A. A.D.S.S./Forms/C. 2118.

WAR DIARY
INTELLIGENCE SUMMARY
(Erase heading not required.)

Army Form C. 2118

JANUARY 1919

Place	Date	Hour	Summary of Events and Information	Remarks and references to Appendices
NIEURLET	1		Fine day. D.A.D.V.S. inspected all animals of H.Q. Nos 2 & 3 sections and classified them according to age and efficiency in A, B & C groups. CAPT B.C. HARDY left proceeding on leave.	JWSJk
"	2		Fine day. CAPT HARRY SMITH proceeded in command of No 3 section to STEEN VORDE. D.A.D.V.S. classified all animals of No 1 section.	JWSJk
"	3		Fine day. Salvage carried out – No 2 section commenced to make horse standings from bricks drawn from ARMY BRICKWORKS HOULLE.	JWSJk
"	4		Fine day. C.R.A. inspected D.A.C. and addressed men on demobilization, re-enlistment & education.	JWSJk
"	5		Fine day. 1 Coal Miner & 1 Long Service Man demobilized. Salvage carried out.	JWSJk
"	6		Fine day. R.O.D Engine crashed into bridge & blocked up Canal passage near ST MOMELIN.	JWSJk
"	7		Fine morning No 2 section from having bricks brought by barge much move their standings. 1 Prussian Guard demobilized.	JWSJk
"	8		Fine day – Salvage carried out. Horse standings previously occupied by No 3 section filled in at ground level from Dull – Corps Horsemaster COL MOSELEY-LEIGH & CAPT CLUTTERBUCK groups all animals into X, Y & Z troops for demobilization.	JWSJk
"	9		Fine – Two men demobilized – Lieut J.W. SMITH proceeded to join II Corps in GERMANY	Henry JWSJk

WAR DIARY or INTELLIGENCE SUMMARY

Army Form C. 2118

JANUARY 1919

Place	Date	Hour	Summary of Events and Information	Remarks and references to Appendices
NIEURLET	10		Fine day – Salving carried out – 12 men demobilized.	NTD
"	11		Fine day – 14 men demobilized.	NTD
"	12		First day – 16 men demobilized – Salvage continued.	NTD
"	13		Fine day – Education started again in D.A.C. under supervision of 2/Lt J.W. BLAIR.	NTD
"	14		Showery – Permission obtained to use sleeping from line being demolished near here by R.C.E.s for building horse standings.	NTD
"	15		Showery – Salvage carried out	NTD
"	16		Fine – Another large load of bricks brought from ARMY BRICKWORKS.	NTD
"	17		Fine – Salvage carried out – LIEUT J. INGLIS despatched for demobilization. MAJOR A.C. GRONCELL M.C. rode over to TILQUES to give evidence in Court martial. 15 men demobilized.	NTD
"	18		14 men demobilized, mostly to SHORNCLIFFE.	NTD
"	19		4 men demobilized – CAPT JENKINS returned to No 2 Section from 159 Bde – LIEUT A.G.J CAMPBELL proceeded to ENGLAND on leave.	NTD
"	20		Fine – very frosty – Roads hard – 2/LIEUT J.W BLAIR proceed for demobilization.	NTD
"	21		Fine – not so cold – 20 men demobilized. MAJOR A.C. GRONCELL MC & CAPT CASSIDY R.A.M.C. went by car to visit No 3 Section at VLAMERTINGHE.	NTD
"	22		Thawing – Overcast – 30 men demobilized – Salvage carried out.	NTD

WAR DIARY
INTELLIGENCE SUMMARY
(Erase heading not required.)

Army Form C. 2118

JANUARY 1919

Place	Date	Hour	Summary of Events and Information	Remarks and references to Appendices
NIEURLET	23		Fine – Freezing hard – Salvage carried out.	WD/S/L
"	24		Fine – Freezing hard – V.O. mallined all 2 grey animals – 5 men demobilised.	WD/S/L
"	25		Dull – Freezing hard – CAPT REPEN proceeded on leave – LIEUT D.H URQUHART sent to No 1 Section. 2 men demobilised.	WD/S/L
"	26		Cloudy – Thaw during day – Freezing hard at night – CAPT HALLETT R.A.M.C. joined for duty – 11 men demobilised.	WD/S/L
"	27		Fine – Thawed in afternoon – C.R.A inspected No 2 Section's lines and expressed himself pleased with the stabling accommodation etc.	WD/S/L
"	28		Fine – Cold – CAPT CASSIDY M.T R.A.M.C. proceeded to ENGLAND on duty. 12 men demobilised.	WD/S/L
"	29		Frosty – Salvage carried out – 4 Newar huts drawn for No 2 Section from WATTEN	WD/S/L
"	30		Very hard frost – Roads very slippery – Salvage continued.	WD/S/L
"	31		Dull & frosty – Orders received to send all blind animals tomorrow to the collecting station ARQUES. Orders received that Divisional Medium Trench Mortars would be affiliated to the D.A.C. before February 8.	WD/S/L

Harry T Smith
Lt RFA

Army Form C. 2118.

WAR DIARY
INTELLIGENCE SUMMARY.
(Erase heading not required.)

35 Divisional Ammunition Column.

Royal Field Artillery.

From 1st February 1919
to 28th February 1919.

Volume 37.

[signature] Major, R.F.A.
COMDG. 35th DIV. AMM. COLUMN.

Army Form C. 2118.

WAR DIARY
INTELLIGENCE SUMMARY. FEBRUARY 1919

(Erase heading not required.)

Instructions regarding War Diaries and Intelligence Summaries are contained in F. S. Regs., Part II. and the Staff Manual respectively. Title pages will be prepared in manuscript.

Place	Date	Hour	Summary of Events and Information	Remarks and references to Appendices
NIEURLET	1		Snowing in the morning. 19 plus animals sent to collecting station ARQUES for sale at COURTRAI	A7511
	2		Very frosty – Extra newin huts being put up at No 2 Section	A7511
	3		Freezing hard – Salvage carried out	A7511
	4		MAJOR A.C. GRUNCELL proceeded on leave to ROUEN. Lieut R.F.P. HEAVENS – TREWMAN proceeded on 14 days special leave to ENGLAND. CAPTAIN M.G. JENKINS assumed Command in absence of MAJOR GRUNCELL	A7511
	5		Thawed in morning – Snowed heavily in evening – Salvage carried out	A7511
	6		Snow 3" deep – Roads very slippery – Slight thaw in afternoon. D.M.T.M. Batteries affiliated to the D.A.C. + attached to No 1 Section. All stores taken over by D.A.C. and two T.M. storemen attached CAPTAIN WHITEHEAD LIEUT SPALDING & 2/LT M.A.H. TINKER attached to No 1 Section. CAPT BARRACLOUGH took over demobilization officer to 35" D.A.C.	A7511
	7		Slight thaw – Roads very bad – 11 men sent for demobilization to KINROSS, PREESHEATH & FOVANT	A7511
	8		Freezing very hard – Roads impassable – Recount of all animals ordered – 17 men despatched for demobilization to KINROSS, PREESHEATH, FOVANT. 2 to KINROSS 3 to GEORGETOWN.	A7511 A7511
	9		Several degrees of frost	A7511
	10		Freezing very hard – Salvage carried out	A7511

Henry Evans Lt. R.T.A.

Army Form C. 2118.

WAR DIARY
INTELLIGENCE SUMMARY.

(Erase heading not required.)

FEBRUARY 1919

Place	Date	Hour	Summary of Events and Information	Remarks and references to Appendices
NIEURLET	11		Hard frost - Good weather - Lieut CAMPBELL rejoined No 2 Section from leave	APPX 1
	12		Still freezing - Bright day - MAJOR N.C. BRUNSELL returned from leave in FRANCE and resumed command of the D.A.C. CAPT F REPEN returned from leave in ENGLAND & resumed command of No 1 Section. LIEUT CAMPBELL admitted to No 4 STATIONARY HOSPITAL with influenza. 2/LT M.A.H TINCKER came to H.Q. D.A.C.	APPX 2
	13		Freezing - Bright day - Orders received to take on the D.A.C. fighting strength 150 Indians formerly attached for instruction.	APPX 3
	14		Mist & cold - Lieut D.H. URQUHART and 2 N.C.O.s proceeded to General Indian Base Depot MARSEILLES to conduct 25 Indians to No 3 Section these Indians were formerly intended for Army Field Brigade Ammunition Columns	APPX 4 APPX 5
	15		Commenced thawing	
	16		Mild - Raining - Thaw precautions adopted. C.R.A & MAJOR A.C GRUNSELL proceeded to VLAMERTINGHE to inspect No 3 Section. Sub to Concentration Camps KINROSS & GEORGETOWN ?	APPX 6
	17		Thawing fast - sunny & quite warm - Salving resumed -	APPX 3
	18		Dull day - Veterinary Officer Lieut Crawford inspected No 2 Sections Animals.	APPX 4
	19		Dull day - 8 men to RIPON sent for disposal. 41 Z class animals proceeded for disposal to ARQUES	APPX 1

Henry J Field Capt R.F.A.

Army Form C. 2118.

WAR DIARY
INTELLIGENCE SUMMARY.
(Erase heading not required.)

FEBRUARY 1919.

No. III

Place	Date	Hour	Summary of Events and Information	Remarks and references to Appendices
NIEURLET	19 (contd)		Animal Collecting Camp. Two mules evacuated to Mobile Veterinary Section	AFC2118
	20		Fine day — Commenced storing harness after disinfection, being rubbed with olubbin and having several jibbs rubbed dry steel work. Sent for demobilization to Concentration Camp for following areas 1 Daventry, 6 Ovenstry, 6 Prestwich	AFC2118
	21		Cloudy & rainy — Lieut R.P.H. TICEHMAN returned from leave in U.K. Sent for demobilization to Concentration Camp 2 Chieldon, 2 Horninky, 4 Purfleet	AFC2118
	22		Very rainy & windy — Salvage unable to be carried out — Unit is now down to cadre strength in personnel excluding Natives & re-enlisted men	AFC2118
	23		Cloudy — 10 Z Class mules sent to ARQUES COLLECTING CAMP by No 2 Section	AFC2118
	24		Fine — Very mild — Salvage continued	AFC2118
	25		Cloudy & Rainy — 66 Z Class mules of "X" Class forwarded under Lieut G. WEBSTER to ARQUES COLLECTING CAMP	AFC2118
	26		Rainy — 8 Riders & 118 Mules of J Class forwarded under Lieut G. WEBSTER to STEENVORDE to exchange with corresponding number of Z Class & undersized animals coming from No 3 Section	AFC2118
	27		Cloudy — 40 German prisoners being utilised in erection for moving NISSEN HUTS etc Lieut G. WEBSTER Feby 14 1919	AFC2118
	28		Raining — Orders received for Lieut (A/Capt) F. REPEN to proceed as soon as possible to take over command of a Brigade Ammunition Columns in VI Corps. German prisoners employed in lieu	AFC2118

Henry ?? Capt R.A.N.

35 D.A.

HEADQUARTERS
35 D.A.C.
-1 APR 1919
H/318.

Herewith war diary for month of March. 1919.

Major, R.F.A.
COMDG. 35th DIV. AMM. COLUMN.

Army Form C. 2118.

WAR DIARY
or
INTELLIGENCE SUMMARY.
(Erase heading not required.)

Vol 38

35 Divisional Ammunition Column
Royal Field Artillery
From 1st March 1919
To 31st March 1919

Volume 38

[signature]
Major, R.F.A.
COMDG. 35th DIV. AMM. COLUMN

WAR DIARY or INTELLIGENCE SUMMARY

Army Form C. 2118.

MARCH 1919

Place	Date	Hour	Summary of Events and Information	Remarks and references to Appendices
NIEURLET	1		Raining & Cloudy :- 1 Mule evacuated to 40 Mob't Vet Section. Summer Time adopted.	APPX
"	2		Raining - Despatched to ARMICOL ARQUES 23 Oxen 16 Z.A 127 Mules all Z Class animals. Inspection at EPERLECQUES of all orders sent for special sale as required for Poor Belgian army	APPX
"	3		Raining. German prisoners of war employed by Artisans for salvage & clearing up roads. All harness and equipment being cleaned up. Wild Chestnut tracked. 1 Mule evacuated to 23 Vet Hospital	APPX APPX
"	4		Fine - Salvage carried out.	APPX
"	5		Fine - Salvage carried out.	APPX
"	6		Fine No.1 section despatched 1 mule allotted for cavalry chargers to ARQUES. P.O.W's employed in salvage from & dump salvage work	APPX
"	7		Despatched to ARQUES 3 Oxen 10 L.D and 56 mules all "X" Class and 1 Rider 1 29 and 8 mules to 23 Vet Hospital mostly with ophthalmia. 16 non-returnable muli sent by motor lorry to No.3 section YPRES under Lieut MAHTINEKER LIEUT D.H URQUHART and Lieut CAMPBELL posted to No.3 section	APPX
"	8		Fine but showery. Despatched to ARQUES 5 oxen clipped Y Animals for special sale.	APPX
"	9		Fine, slight showers 21 men from Nos 1 & 2 section posted to Stryng Camps ESQUELBECQ and went there by motor lorry Church Parade	APPX
"	10		Fine, slight showers. Despatched to ARQUES 3 oxen clipped and 2 L.D "Y" animals for special sale in U.K. 6 Native Drivers arrived from Indian Base Depot. 1 Corpl from Rouen from 157 Bde R.F.A. Lieut (A/Capt) J.G WHITE HERD posted to 17 Lancer Traction Salvage of manure etc Lieut N.C HOLDER assumes command Nov 1918. Henry WENGA Capt R.F.A	APPX

WAR DIARY
INTELLIGENCE SUMMARY

Army Form C. 2118.

MARCH 1919

Place	Date	Hour	Summary of Events and Information	Remarks and references to Appendices
NIEURLET	11		Fine – Cpl. M.T. Dunn posted to 159 Bde R.F.A. to relieve Cpl. Bowyer from B/159 R.F.A.	
"	12		Fine dirt drill – 5 men to A STAGING CAMP	
"	13		Fine – No 1831 Gnr. WESTCOTT proceeded to join Grand Rhine Army – 171 Ammunition boxes co. for 4.5 ammunition received.	
"	14		Raining – Trench Mortar Carriages returned to ORDNANCE in accordance with G.R.O. 6144.	
"	15		Dull – 7"Z" M/Ms to ARMICOL ARQUES. Capt. F. Rolow "X" Charges to ARMICOL. No grease addressed to H.Q. D.A.C. COLOGNE. Notice received that No 3 section will be returning shortly from YPRES to form a 2 New Depot at FORGES-LES-EAUX will all non-reliable personnel and Indian personnel.	
"	16		Dull – One "X" animal decapitated to ARMICOL ARQUES. – Church Parade (R.C.)	
"	17		Dull – Salvage carried out – Demobilized sent for disposal 8 men.	
"	18		Fine showery. Orders received that General Demobilization has been ordered and instructions as regards proceeding to U.K. of earlier Intro – section football completion. No 1 beat No 2 H.Q. 4 – 2	
"	19		Fine – Salvage carried out by sections – 357 Other ranks posted to B.A.C. from Brigades to make up cadre of No 3 section but have not yet joined.	
"	20		During the moment shirt time in afternoon – Salvage carried out – Instructions D.A.D. O.d. that he acts as the S.D.M. will inspect all M.T. stores in accordance with Army Demob Regulations & Instructions	
"	21		Dull & cloudy – Salvage carried out	
"	22		Dull & showery – Orders received that all demobilization orders leave to Cadre personnel carried out will further notice till further instructions are received of return to ENGLAND	

Henry Smith Capt. R.F.A.

SHEET 27 M.114 D

WAR DIARY or INTELLIGENCE SUMMARY.

Army Form C. 2118.

MARCH 1919

Place	Date	Hour	Summary of Events and Information	Remarks and references to Appendices
NIEPPE	23		Fine - cold - Wire received that previous order re application of demobilization having been cancelled Capt HARRY SMITH returns with No.3 Section from POTIJZE (YPRES) and Lieut. D.W.H. JOHNSON and 1/c M.A.H. TINCKER. Two X riders deputated to 3rd Div Signal Coy. Ben X rider to Area Commandant BOLLEZEELE. 194 MULES and 1 Rider and X Bren inspection.	14/3/19
"	24		to AGRICOL ARRIVES. Dull cloudy - Disbanded and went for march to area IX-A. 1 Gunner + 1 Driver reported for Z Wire Dept. from 30th Div. Arty also 1 NCO and 11 Native drivers. E.O. inspected all personnel, equipment + clothing of No.1 section and D.M.T.M. affiliated to that section.	15/3/19
"	25		Fine - freezing. Inspection by E.O. of No.2 section personnel, equipment, clothing + transport No.2 section.	16/3/19
"	26		Fine - milder - Inspection by E.O. of J.N.R. personnel + equipment. Capt R.M. CHALKLEY joined from D/159 Bde. R.F.A. to take over No.3 section when Capt H SMITH proceeds to Z/1st Div DAC. 9 N.C.O.S. and T.O.M. inspected all U.S. stores, equipment + vehicles of all sections and discharged before the AF B104s in respect of receiving a copy for each section.	17/3/19
"	27		Intermittent showers + sunshine - Native coolies sent for hire - C.R.E. drew timber for erection to pay goodbye to section Commanders who he left for ENGLAND.	18/3/19
"	28		Snowing hard - 3 inches deep on the ground	19/3/19
"	29			
"	30		At times very fine then snowing and hailing (Church Parade R.C.)	20/3/19
"	31		Fine - Salvage proceeded with. Orders received that all animals must remain near their billets and camps until further orders.	21/3/19

SHEET 27 M 14 d

Manzie
Capt R.F.A

WAR DIARY

35th DIVISIONAL AMMUNITION COLUMN, R.F.A.

M A R C H

1 9 1 8

WAR DIARY

INTELLIGENCE SUMMARY.

(Erase heading not required.)

Army Form C. 2118.

Vol 26

SECRET

35th DIVISIONAL AMMUNITION COLUMN.

From 1st MARCH 1918
To 31st MARCH 1918

VOLUME 26

T. Bowman
Lt Col.
Cmdg. 35 D.A.C. R.F.A.

Army Form C. 2118.

WAR DIARY
INTELLIGENCE SUMMARY.
(Erase heading not required.)

MARCH 1918

Instructions regarding War Diaries and Intelligence Summaries are contained in F.S. Regs., Part II. and the Staff Manual respectively. Title pages will be prepared in manuscript.

Place	Date	Hour	Summary of Events and Information	Remarks and references to Appendices
ROUSSEL FARM	1st		Weather Showery. Lt TREWMAN proceeded on leave to UK. BQMS LIFFORD proceeded on one months leave to UK under G.R.O. 14. O.R. proceeded on leave to UK	Plt
	2nd		Weather very cold. Snow in afternoon. Lt CROSSLEY posted to T.M. Battery. Lt PLAYLE joined from base & was posted to No. 1 Section	Plt
	3rd		Church parade	Plt
	4th		Work on Army & Corps line Gun positions carried on	Plt
	5th		30 O.R. joined from base	Plt
	6th		Above work Continued (4) also agricultural work carried on	Plt
	7th		Capt. WILKINSON returned from leave in UK. Above fatigues carried on (4th & 5th)	Plt
	8th		Capt WILKINSON assumed Command of the Column. Capt BARNETT took over duties of Adjutant. Usual fatigues carried on Army Line positions & agriculture. Weather very fine	Plt
	9th		Very fine day. Lt. Col. MACKINSON I. Cohs horse Master inspected all animals & expressed himself as very satisfied with conditions of same. [Contd]	Plt

MAP Sheet 28 B13a 3.7
BELGIUM
ELVERDINGHE

WAR DIARY

INTELLIGENCE SUMMARY

Army Form C. 2118.

MARCH 1918

(Erase heading not required.)

Place	Date	Hour	Summary of Events and Information	Remarks and references to Appendices
ROUSSEZ FARM Mont Black 28 B 12 a 9.1 ELVERDINGHE BELGIUM	9th (Contd)		LICHFIELD DUMP. Handed over to 1st Divn Stores BARDS. CAUSEWAY BOMB STORES WOLVERTON DUMP.	Apx
	10th		Capt SMITH proceeded on leave to U.K.	Apx
	11th		Received orders to hold ourselves ready to entrain at 24 hours notice. Weather still very fine	Apx
			11 Col. D.E. FORMAN returned from 159 Bde. & took over Command of the Column. Notice of move reduced to 12 hours. to REPEN took charge of D.A. working	Apx
	12th		Party on Army Gypho line Gun positions at Canal Bank	Apx
	13th		Working parties carried on. Weather fine	Apx
	14th		Weather wet. Working parties carried on	Apx
	15th		Fine day. Received orders to proceed to CROMBEEK on 16th MARCH.	Apx
			Orders to move cancelled as camp at CROMBEEK was very poor.	Apx
	16th		Weather fine. Work on A & C June positions carried on	Apx

Signed

WAR DIARY

INTELLIGENCE SUMMARY

Army Form C. 2118.

MARCH 1918

(Erase heading not required.)

Place	Date	Hour	Summary of Events and Information	Remarks and references to Appendices
ROUSSEL FARM (Map Sheet 28 Rise S.I.) ELVERDINGHE BELGIUM	17th		Lt. CHAMBERS proceeded on leave to U.K. Army Commander expressed his appreciation of the good work carried out on BATTLE LINE defences, to all ranks concerned	PM
	18th		No.1 Section Camp shelled with H.V. Gun, no damage done. Weather fine.	PM
	19th		Weather fine. Camp again shelled no casualties	PM
	20th		Weather fine.	PM
	21st		Lt. TREWMAN returned from leave in U.K. Camp again shelled without damage being in photo. Weather fine. Camp again shelled. Lt HARRINGTON proceeded on leave to U.K. Received orders to be ready to entrain midnight 22/23rd March. Working parties rejoined Column.	PM
	22nd		orders received to entrain night of 23/24th March. Weather fine.	PM
	23rd		HQ Marched out from ROUSSEEL FARM at 11. A.M. & proceeded to PROVEN via Switch road, entrained at PROVEN [CONT'D]	PM

WAR DIARY
INTELLIGENCE SUMMARY

Army Form C. 2118.

MARCH 1918

Place	Date	Hour	Summary of Events and Information	Remarks and references to Appendices
23 [Entry]	23	6 PM	No 1 Section att. to HQ & K Batteries 157 Bde Entrained at PESELHOEK. No 2 " " " " 157 Bde " " " No 3 " " " " 159 Bde " at ROUSBROUGE Weather fine. Entrained " " PROVEN	
Sht 62D 2.25a	24th		HQ detrained at HEILLY 7 PM & Marched to ETINEHEM. No 1 Section detrained at CORBIE & Marched to CHIPILLY No 2 " " " MERICOURT L'ABBE & Marched KETINEHEM	
Sht 62D Q 4a	25th		Less HQ Column assembled at CHIPILLY in the Chateau grounds. Weather remained fine. Received orders Midnight 25/6 to retire. Cancelled later & ttd to remain at CHIPILLY.	
Sht 62D 57.A V25a	26		H.Q. moved to CERISY 7.45 AM. arriving there 4.30 AM. A echelon proceeded to VAUX-SUR-SOMME during ammunition from the dumps there & delivering it to batteries at MORLANCOURT × roads on the BRAY-CORBIE road. B echelon marched direct to LAVIEVILLE & thence WARLOY where they were joined by HQ & No 2 Section. No trace of No 1 Section. Ammunition ordered by K157 Bde killed in action. No 1 Section Joined ammd WARLOY 6 PM. Lorries refilled at VECQUEMONT, & remained there night 26/27	
ditto	27th		Weather fine	

R.C.Anderson Lt RFA

Army Form C. 2118.

WAR DIARY
or
INTELLIGENCE SUMMARY.   MARCH 1918.
(Erase heading not required.)

Place	Date	Hour	Summary of Events and Information	Remarks and references to Appendices
Skelly D V:50 a	28th		Fine in Morning, rain in afternoon. Orders received probably move to FRECHENCOURT area about 29th. Lt REPEN assumed Command of No.1 Section. Capt. WILKINSON attached VII Corps.	P.H.
	29th		Dull weather. Orders received to move on 30th to FRECHENCOURT.	P.H.
Sept D. 62 B 30 a & c	30th		Left WARLOY 10.15 AM arrived FRECHENCOURT 1.30 PM. Camped in open no billets available in village. Very heavy rain.	P.H.
ditto	31st		H.Q. moved into billet in FRECHENCOURT. Weather dull.	P.H. Pennington

www.ingramcontent.com/pod-product-compliance
Lightning Source LLC
Chambersburg PA
CBHW080846230426

43662CB00013B/2032